# LUTHER AND PHILOSOPHIES OF THE REFORMATION

ALSO AVAILABLE FROM BLOOMSBURY

*Effort and Grace,* Simone Kotva

*The Promise of Martin Luther's Political Theology,* Michael Richard Laffin

*Reflections on Reformational Theology,* Kimlyn J. Bender

# LUTHER AND PHILOSOPHIES OF THE REFORMATION

Edited by Boris Gunjević

BLOOMSBURY ACADEMIC
LONDON • NEW YORK • OXFORD • NEW DELHI • SYDNEY

BLOOMSBURY ACADEMIC
Bloomsbury Publishing Plc
50 Bedford Square, London, WC1B 3DP, UK
1385 Broadway, New York, NY 10018, USA
29 Earlsfort Terrace, Dublin 2, Ireland

BLOOMSBURY, BLOOMSBURY ACADEMIC and the Diana logo are trademarks of
Bloomsbury Publishing Plc

First published in Great Britain 2023
Paperback edition published 2024

Cover design by Ben Anslow
Cover images: Handwritten text with The Song of the Nibelungs (c.13th century)
(© Grafissimo / Getty Images);
Close up portrait of a Great Horned Owl (© GeorgePeters / Getty Images);
Luther Rose and Luther's sign for printings. Wood engravings after an
original of 1529, published in 1879. (© ZU_09 / Getty Images)

A catalogue record for this book is available from the British Library.

A catalog record for this book is available from the Library of Congress.

ISBN:   HB:      978-1-3502-1405-7
        PB:      978-1-3502-1408-8
        ePDF:    978-1-3502-1404-0
        eBook:   978-1-3502-1406-4

Typeset by RefineCatch Limited, Bungay, Suffolk

To find out more about our authors and books visit www.bloomsbury.com
and sign up for our newsletters.

# CONTENTS

# PREFACE – LUTHER AND PHILOSOPHIES OF THE REFORMATION

## *Simon Perry*

Historians are inevitably and inescapably ventriloquists, subconsciously stuffing their words into the mouths of those without the ability to answer back. Few great figures from the past have attracted more attention from the finest and most passionate ventriloquists than an Augustinian monk from Eisleben. Even with the most generous spirit and conscientious rigour, academics and church leaders alike who gaze upon Martin Luther – be it with disdain or awe – face the danger of reducing him to a sock-puppet who voices opinions that they may subsequently denounce or applaud. Given his voluminous writing and outspoken style, it is perfectly possible for modern readers to reconstruct any number of mutually inconsistent Luthers – all of them faithful to the reformer's own writings. Thankfully, although ventriloquism is inevitable it is also limited by a historian's readiness to make 'known things unknown'. That is, to allow what we already 'know for sure' about the subject to be exposed to critique and if necessary, abandoned, forgotten and un-known.

All of this may be readily accepted by many historians today, but the sheer difficulty of this task may not always be fully appreciated. Trust in the safety mechanisms of the academy is no substitute for the historian's readiness to subject themselves to the harrowing personal experience of 're-formation'. For instance, a multidisciplinary conference might serve the admirable role of allowing multiple dimensions of expertise to highlight elements of history that had long been 'unknown'. Equally, a multidisciplinary conference might serve only to establish a more efficient means of unearthing a modern Luther, an 'object' of study who does not speak unless spoken to. The present volume achieves almost the exact opposite. The collective work of contributors portrays a Luther who might just force his own words back into the mouth of the attentive ventriloquist.

The volume is the outcome of a conversation and reflection whose tone was distinctive, characterized by a tangible desire to hear Martin Luther. To hear, not simply as the capacity to process new information, so much as the willingness to make room for the other. To know not more about what we already know, so much as to rehabilitate our knowledge – with the hope that we learned to *re-cognize* Luther. This is no easy task for a character as complex and courageous as the great *Re-former* himself. In the turbulence of his day, it was perfectly plausible to be borne by the unfettered rage arising from gentle care, the surges of sheer hatred generated by profound political love, and the outrageous audacity rooted in self-abasing humility. Luther's own hand betrays traits reprehensible to many, and from which he cannot be absolved – as well as traits of such ethical depth as to be unparalleled by even the most unwittingly self-righteous moral police post-modernity can muster. He exhibited both profound concern for the other, and a spirit of outright racism; both an astounding capacity for painstaking moral reflection and a reckless impulsivity; both a terrifying resistance to long-treasured ideological comfort and a pathetic complicity to prevailing moral norms. Portraits that demonise or deify this figure have all thus, not surprisingly, gained much traction in contemporary discourse.

Luther himself would have something to say about nature of the late capitalist discourse that quietly predetermines the shape of contemporary Lutheran idols and icons. (Usually an ethically deodorized inspiration who leaves the political, economic and social spheres untouched, a hero of the 'feisty but spineless' pedigree). The nature of our discourse seemed very much in the mind of the book editor who was careful to create an environment Boris

Gunjevic describes using Foucault's notion of a 'heterotopia', a place in which one may encounter genuine space of suppressed knowledge of otherness. A book is always ideally such a space, a meeting of those who are 'brought' (*ferre*) 'together' (*con*). However, this does not mean that delegates merely share the same psycho-geographical location. Like members of a synagogue (lit. those who are 'led together') they bring with them the readiness to engage with that which might be genuinely 'other'. A healthy theological and philosophical discourse might best be understood in these terms: a space in which those in *attendance* expect to *attend* to that which is other, to experience heterotopia. If we are to hear Luther above the voice of our own ventriloquism, such a space may well be a necessity.

Each of the authors exemplified brilliantly the otherness of a healthy reflection, both in terms of the content of presentations and the interactions that followed. Prof. John Barclay's work on grace, in all its social, economic, and spiritual fullness, compels us to re-asses not only the dynamics of grace as revealed in scripture, but (via the New Finnish reading) reveals facets of Lutheran thought that invite further reflection. Prof. Morna Hooker offers a critically affirming response, re-reading Paul's epistles through the lenses provided by her former student. Prof. Robin Kirkpatrick reminds us that Luther did not burst into history like a rabbit from a hat – outlining instead how Dante had long since penned severe critiques of Medieval Christendom. Though Dante's concerns and proposals differ from Luther's, Kirkpatrick reveals how they draw from a common tradition of critique. Prof. Robert Rosin draws attention to the enchanted but misguided certainties that commemorations of Luther can engender. A shift of focus to the 'priesthood of all believers' reminds us that – in Luther's thought – necessities of structure and procedure never take precedence over the community's principle responsibility to hear God. Prof. Robert Kolb re-visits the ecclesiastical context and consequence of Luther's activities, highlighting the fundamental role of Scripture as the word-made-flesh in the local congregation. Prof. Slavoj Zizek's account plots an entirely different path, heralding Luther as a heroic and necessary forerunner to Hegel and Marx. Zizek's notion of 'Christian atheism' presents a serious challenge to both atheist and Christian, daring them to face head-on the disturbance and trauma represented by the other. Finally, Prof. John Milbank emphasises the profound relevance of Reformation today. He offers a radically alternative account of how the negative forces of Modernity and Capitalism arise from the malformed ideologies promulgated by a misdirected reformation Christianity.

The presentations compiled in the present volume, together constitute a literary heterotopia. The multi-faceted character of Luther is not reduced to a homogenous, one-dimensional historical figure but affirmed as a full-blooded character whose wide-ranging interests, concerns and contradictions are clearly laid out. The final result here is a book that requires much of the reader. Different chapters encourage us to make connections between heterogeneous elements of focus. The connections we would make between the different portrayals force us to strain our ears to hear how the great re-former might reveal himself *through* those connections. It is by such means that Luther may escape our objectification to become a conversation partner. It is an invitation to encounter re-formation in the core of one's being. Though Luther's voice will of course remain unpredictable at a conscious level, he may nevertheless interrupt our own inner deliberations and interpretations. Ventriloquism is not, as Stanley Fish would say, 'the only game in town'.

This literary heterotopia makes room for the sixteenth-century theologian to view our world through our eyes (as we are forced to re-view our place in that world), to deliberate on our predicaments (as we are compelled to theological re-flection), and so to put his words in our mouth (as we encounter re-formation as a personal experience).

# 1

# Luther, Paul, and Gift

*John M.G. Barclay*

The three terms in my chapter title represent the intersection of two significant debates of the last few decades. On the one hand, the question of Luther and Paul; on the other, debates on the meaning and significance of the gift. Starting in the 1960s and reaching a crescendo in the 'new perspective' on Paul, a chorus of voices has condemned Luther as a poor interpreter of Paul: Luther's 'introspective conscience', his individualism, his reading of the faith-works antithesis, his law-gospel polarity, and his construal of Jews and Judaism – all these and more have been condemned as a misconstrual of Paul that has infected the whole Protestant exegetical tradition for 500 years.[1] This is not entirely new: significant figures in New Testament scholarship, such as F.C. Baur, W. Wrede, and A. Schweitzer previously distanced themselves from key elements of their Lutheran heritage in reading Paul, but the shift in the consensus in the last generation has been without precedent. We could name a number of factors: for some scholars, the turn against Bultmann and his legacy was enough to discredit the Luther on whose shoulders Bultmann stood; for others, 'Luther' has been a cipher for the whole Western theological tradition (stretching back to Augustine), which is generally considered guilty of misreading Paul through the filter of later Christian dogma; for others again, our post-Holocaust context makes it impossible to represent Judaism as a religion of works-righteousness, so that any Lutheran reading retrojected onto Paul's arguments sounds like anti-Judaism.[2] In general, with the demise of Bultmann's theological interpretation, New Testament scholars reverted to a rigorous, not to say positivistic, commitment to historical readings of Paul, in which reconstructions of Paul's social context accompanied a deep distrust of the history of reception. The Protestant call *ad fontes* was here turned against the Reformers themselves: Paul should be viewed on his own original terms, not 'through Reformation spectacles'.[3] When one combines that approach with widespread ignorance of Luther's works, the stage is set for a deeply unsympathetic reception of Luther. Because Luther did not match our own expectations of a historical critic, his theological engagement with Paul and his subtle recontextualization of Paul's gospel for his sixteenth-century audience were disparaged as a misreading. There are signs now of a refusal to let this disparagement have the last word, with New Testament scholars such as Stephen Chester and Jonathan Linebaugh making us ask whether Luther might, after all, have something to teach us about Paul.[4] I am glad the Luther-Jahr has encouraged us to consider that possibility afresh.

The other debate to which my title draws attention is the widespread discussion of gift in anthropology and history that has taken place over the last 100 years and has been prominent in the last two decades in the fields of philosophy and theology. Jacques Derrida, Jean-Luc Marion, Kathryn Tanner, and John Milbank all spring to mind immediately here, but more widely it seems that almost every continental philosopher or theologian worth her or his salt has had something to say on this topic.[5] Interestingly, Luther has not been much discussed in this context – or if discussed, only critically so – although Paul has sometimes figured in recent European philosophy. If Luther's theology of gift stands behind some modern understandings of 'charity' and 'altruism', Luther deserves more careful attention in this matter than he has so far attracted.[6]

# 1. The gift in Luther

'When you lay hold of Christ as a gift that is given you for your very own, and have no doubt about it, you are a Christian'.[7] That sentence sums up in characteristic terms the core of Luther's theology of gift. The gift is, first and foremost, Christ himself (not something given by Christ, but Christ himself), even if Luther in the Catechisms will apply the gift language also to all three persons of the Trinity. And Christ is always and exclusively *gift*: as Luther puts it elsewhere, 'Christ is not Moses, not a taskmaster or a lawgiver; He is the Dispenser of grace, the Savior, and the Pitier. In other words, he is nothing but sheer, infinite mercy, which gives and is given'.[8] In instructing readers on how to read the Gospels, Luther is at pains to insist that before he is an example, Christ is a gift, the manifestation of the 'great fire of the love of God for us, whereby the heart and conscience become happy, secure and content'.[9] That gift 'is given you for your very own', says Luther, in words that echo Paul (Galatians 2.20) and whose personal, existential, and affective tone were hallmarks of Luther's theology and subsequently of Protestantism.[10] 'Laying hold of Christ as gift' and 'having no doubt' are expressions for faith – not a condition for the gift to be given, but the mode in which the gift is received. And that is *all* that is required, according to Luther, to be a Christian. Works will follow, as fruit is borne by the tree, but the person is created and secured in this simplest and most profound way: by receiving the gift of Christ, and thus forgiveness, justification, freedom, and salvation in him.

Gift and grace are not always synonyms for Luther: he learned via Melanchthon (who gained this from Erasmus), that *charis* in Greek generally means 'favour' and expresses in Paul God's favourable disposition towards the world in Christ, not an entity infused into the believer (as in some medieval understandings of *gratia*).[11] Following Romans 5.15, he could draw a distinction between 'grace' and 'gift', as in his treatise *Against Latomus* (1521), though in many cases *Gnade* and *Gabe* overlap enough to be practically synonymous.[12]

What both express for Luther is that God comes to the world in Christ, in baptism, in the Supper, and in the preaching of the gospel, in the mode of gift. For whatever might be one's initial impression from reading the Gospels, 'the gospel is really not a book of laws and commandments, which requires deeds of us, but a book of divine promises in which God promises, offers, and gives us all his possessions and benefits in Christ'.[13] That, we might say, is a characteristically Pauline frame for hermeneutics.

But, of course, gifts are of many different sorts, and may be given for many reasons. The essential thing for Luther is that the gift is free, given without regard to merit or worth. In one sense, this was hardly original: all theologians could agree that Christ came to call 'not the righteous, but sinners' (Mark 2.17) and that Christ 'died for the ungodly' (Romans 5.6). What was distinctive but crucial in Luther was the insistence that this incongruity marks not just the beginning of the Christian life, but the whole of it, that merit or worth have no part in salvation, beginning, middle, or end, and that right to the last (as he put it in a note found by his deathbed) 'we are beggars, *hoc est verum*'.[14] This *permanent incongruity*, this lifelong mismatch between grace and the worth of the believer, famously summarized in the paradoxical slogan, *simul justus et peccator*, is for Luther essential to the understanding of the love of God and the gift of Christ. In the words of the famous final thesis of the Heidelberg Disputation, 'the love of God does not find, but create that which is pleasing to it'.[15] Thus, the love of God 'loves sinners, evil persons, fools and weaklings in order to make them righteous, good, wise and strong'. Crucially, however, they are made righteous, good, and strong not in themselves, but in Christ, that is, by being joined to *his* righteousness, goodness, wisdom, and strength.[16] Luther's favourite metaphor for this 'joining' is marriage, where what belongs to the bridegroom (Christ) may be said to belong also to the bride, but it is notable that he turns to this image with reference not only to Ephesians 5 but also to Hosea 1–2, with the believer figured as the prostitute-made-wife, who brings nothing to the marriage except her own sin.[17] There is here what Luther calls a 'happy exchange' (*froehliche Wechsel*), but it is not that believers brings some *good* to this relationship which contributes to its shared delight; rather, Christ takes upon himself our sin, and we draw from Christ his righteousness, holiness, and life. As Luther puts it, in his *Freedom of a Christian*,

> Christ is full of grace, life and salvation. The soul is full of sins, death, and damnation. Now let faith come between them and sins, death, and damnation will be Christ's, while grace, life, and salvation will be the soul's; for if Christ is a bridegroom he must take upon himself the things which are his bride's, and bestow upon her the things that are his'.[18]

In this sense, the Christian life, while continually active in good works, is at its base a *vita passiva*, a 'receptive life'.[19] To live by faith is to live in perpetual receipt of the gift.

For Luther, to be a recipient of the gift is also to be its conduit. To receive the gift of God in Christ, and to be freed of the concern to gain this gift by good works, is at the same time to be freed to pass it on to others, to 'pay it forward' in service to our neighbours. This structure of theology and ethics, freedom and service is the structure of Luther's *Freedom of the Christian*, surely the best short summary of Luther's thought. Loving service of the neighbour is liberated from the concern to win the favour of God, since the believer is confident in having all good things already in Christ. Luther constructs the Christian reasoning thus:

> Although I am an unworthy and condemned man, my God has given me in Christ all the riches of righteousness and salvation, without any merit on my part, out of pure, free mercy, so that from now on I need nothing except faith which believes that this is true. Why should I not therefore freely, joyfully, with all my heart, and with an eager will do all things I know are pleasing and acceptable to such a Father who has overwhelmed me with his inestimable riches? I will therefore give myself as a Christ to my neighbor, just as Christ offered himself to me; I will do nothing in this life except what

I see is necessary, profitable, and salutary to my neighbor, since through faith I have an abundance of all good things in Christ.[20]

The emphasis on this service being free, willing, spontaneous (*liberaliter, hilariter, spontaneo studio*) is characteristic of Luther, not just for its emotional tone, but for its insistence that this is no grudging obedience to a command, and no obligation required to win some future benefit, but the simple, unforced flow of gift, cascading from God, through the heart of the believer, to the benefit of others.

It is important to pause here, to note the care with which Luther limits any hints of *circularity* in this progress of gift, and the moral tone by which he distinguishes the divine cascade of gift from the self-seeking systems of exchange that he diagnosed in alternative systems of gift and salvation. This feature is variously assessed in contemporary theology, with Luther variously praised or blamed for the ideal of the non-reciprocated gift.[21] It is easy to over-simplify matters. In one sense, it is clear that the gift of God in Christ elicits and enables a response; it is not 'unilateral' if that means it takes effect even where it is unacknowledged. Faith is the basic form of response, and crucial in recognizing God as the sole giver of salvation, acknowledging God as God: the praise and thanksgiving that accompany this faith are thus integral to it.[22] Thus, in Luther's words (just cited), the believer is eager to do what is 'pleasing and acceptable to the Father' – and we may note how this is put in *personal*, familial terms, not as obedience to an impersonal command. In these senses, it would be wrong to say that there is for Luther no 'return' from the believer to God, but this 'return' in faith and love is not best described as a *gift-exchange*, not least as believers have no gifts of their own to give to God. More importantly, it is not intended or able to elicit any further gift or grace from God. In other words, the return is not instrumental, and not designed to continue a cycle of gift and counter-gift, because the one gift has already been given, entire and complete, in Christ. Famously, Luther reconfigured the Mass as a sacrament of receiving, and not as an offering of sacrifice to God, since he wished to avoid any notion that giving *to God* plays some role in our ultimate salvation.

At every point Luther is inclined to present this matter in the form of a straightforward antithesis between giving to others and getting for oneself, the latter represented as a form of selfishness or characterized as a form of barter or commercial exchange. A contrast between gift and (sordid) trade was a trope as old as ancient Greece, but it is important to note that *that* ancient contrast was not between gift-as-non-exchange and trade-as-exchange, but between *two kinds of exchange*, gift-exchange being noble since it was personal, voluntary, and non-calculable, while trade or barter was regarded as impersonal, contractual, and calculating, and generally suspected of 'sharp practice'.[23] Luther adapts this old trope to contrast grace as *non-exchange* with merit as exchange, and thus characterizes the whole theology of merit as sordid, self-seeking exchange – an association aided by the fact that money was often part of the merit-acquiring business (in endowments, masses and, of course, indulgences). In his version of this trope, any form of giving that is not solely and exclusively one-way is characterized as a form of selfishness or low-status barter. This antithetical schema is applied first to God. The God encountered in the gospel 'gives to everyone and takes nothing for what he gives'.[24] By contrast, those who seek God's favour by good works 'want to buy God's grace directly from him with their many good works (as they call them) as if God were a huckster or journeyman who did not want to grant his grace and favour for nothing'.[25] In the thesis from the Heidelberg Disputation cited above (Thesis 28), God's love which 'does not find but create that which is pleasing to it' is contrasted with human love which 'comes into being through that which is pleasing to it'. This antithesis immediately morphs into a contrast between generous giving and selfish receiving: human love 'in all things seeks those things which are its own and receives rather than gives something good', while in the case of God, 'rather than seeking its own good, the love of God flows forth and bestows good'.[26] God's love gives; human love gets. That stark antithesis is backed up by a quote from Acts 20.35, 'It is more blessed to give than to receive'. As Luther puts it concisely in his lectures on the Psalms, 'This is what it means to be God: not to receive but to give good'.[27]

Thus, one of Luther's central criticisms of medieval soteriology is that it constitutes, at a deep level, a mode of seeking one's own good. If sin is, for Luther, humanity as *homo incurvatus in se ipsum*, self-obsessed sinners are not liberated from sin, only further imprisoned, if they are encouraged to think about merit and reward. Scripture, he insists, 'describes man as turned in on himself that he uses not only physical but even spiritual goods for his own purposes, and in all things seeks only himself'.[28] We should love and serve God, Luther insists, for God's own sake, not for reward, but instead 'we are taught by the doctrine of men to seek nothing but merits, rewards, and the things that are ours'; 'in all these things we seek only our profit (*ea quae nostra sunt*), thinking that through them our sins are purged away and that we find salvation in them'.[29] This is a harsh criticism to level against those who thought they were, in fact, pleasing God, by the good works concerned, but once he configures such works as a kind of selfish self-concern, it is easy to represent the Catholic faithful as 'parasites' who fawn on God for their own advantage.[30]

The logic that values giving over getting, and characterizes any desire to get as a form of self-seeking, affects the way Luther depicts giving among humans, that cascade of gift mentioned earlier. Such giving, he insists, should seek no benefit for the giver; since the soul 'has Christ as its righteousness, and therefore seeks only the welfare of others'.[31] One might think that this would apply only to spiritual benefits, but this pattern of thought takes Luther further. 'A man does not live for himself alone in this mortal body, to work for it alone, but he lives also for all men on earth; rather he lives only for others and not for himself' (we may note the slide from 'also' to 'only').[32] Thus Ephesians 4.28 instructs us to work not so we can support ourselves but only so we can give to those in need.[33] Although Luther notes in this context the mutuality in Paul's instruction to 'bear one another's burdens' (Galatians 6.2), the emphasis throughout is on the urge to give, to serve, and to be 'Christ' to one's neighbour, even taking on their sins and weaknesses:

> From love flows a joyful, willing, and free mind that serves one's neighbor willingly and takes no account of gratitude or ingratitude, of praise or blame, of gain or loss. For a man does not serve that he may put men under obligations. He does not distinguish between friends and enemies or anticipate their thankfulness or unthankfulness, but he most freely and willingly spends himself and all that he has, whether he wastes all on the thankless or whether he gains a reward.[34]

In this posture of giving, any 'reward' or 'gain' is entirely incidental; the emphasis lies on the beauty of the one-way, non-circulating gift.

One may surely locate here one root of the distinctively Protestant (but now, through Kant, broadly modern) notion of 'no-return altruism', the ideal of the gift without return, with its stark antithesis between egotistical self-interest and disinterested self-renunciation for the sake of others. Berndt Hamm, as a Lutheran theologian, celebrates in Luther a revolution in the notion of gift: 'what was never anticipated in the history of religions' was 'that there can be any pure, unconditional gift without the giver expecting and receiving from the recipient a reciprocal gift of even the most insignificant or subtle worth whatsoever'.[35] Anders Nygren famously set up a macro-contrast between Eros and Agape, Eros as acquisitive, egocentric, driven by the will to get and possess, Agape as sacrificial, unselfish, free, seeking not to get but to give.[36] For such scholars, this ideal of the non-reciprocated gift is the glory of the Lutheran tradition; for others, such as William Cavanaugh, it constitutes a serious flaw that has accelerated the modern antinomy between gift and exchange, creating a debilitating distinction between private philanthropy and public self-interest.[37] The Derrida-Milbank debate about gift revolves around this issue, though Derrida, in his perfection of the non-reciprocated gift, never acknowledged how much he owed, however distantly, to Luther.

# 2. Luther as interpreter of Paul

Luther grasped something core to Paul's theology in his insistence on the incongruity of grace.[38] In the last generation, Pauline scholars have paid rather little attention to grace, in reaction against 'Lutheran' readings of Paul, and in understandable anxiety lest we reinstate a loaded distinction between Christianity as grace and Judaism (or other religions) as non-grace. But the gift language is central in Paul's statements about the Christ-event (Galatians 1.4; 2.20; 5.4; Romans 3.21–26; 5.6–8, 12–21; 8.32 etc.), which he can summarize in abstract terms as the coming of gift or grace into a cosmos under the power of sin and death (Romans 5.12–21). To abandon Christ is to 'fall from grace' (Galatians 5.4), and to undermine 'the truth of the gospel' (Galatians 2.14) is to reject the grace of God (Galatians 2.21). Both his own 'calling' and the calling of his Gentile converts are described by Paul as a calling in grace (Galatians 1.6, 15; 1 Corinthians 15.9–10). Of course, Paul was not the only person to speak about the grace or the mercy of God, just as Luther was not the only or the first theologian to speak of God's gift or favour. What Luther grasped here in Paul was that this grace bore no relation to worth, was unconditioned by the achievements of its recipients, and was thus an incongruous form of grace. Teasing that out, as the love of God for the unlovely, the weak, and the sinner, was one of Luther's special achievements, and making this real in the lives, consciences, and emotions of his contemporaries has set the tone of Protestantism ever since. Newton's 'Amazing Grace', Methodism's hymns, and the spirituality of hundreds of millions of Protestants around the globe today owe much to this Lutheran reception of Paul's theology of the undeserved gift.

As I have commented elsewhere, in activating this Pauline legacy in the context of the sixteenth century, Luther inevitably altered its focus in key respects.[39] Paul's theology of grace was integral to his mission at the very start of the Christian movement. He took the unconditioned gift of Christ to call into question the regnant systems of worth in both the Jewish and the non-

Jewish environments of his converts. If God's grace is given without regard to worth, it disregards not only achievement or success in good works, but the very criteria of worth by which such works were defined as 'good' – together with the criteria of worth associated with ethnicity, ancestry, gender, education, and legal status. The radicalism of Paul's mission, and its capacity to create experimental communities that crossed social and ethnic boundaries, owed much to this sense that God's gift of Christ – and the accompanying gift of the Spirit – did not accord with the social values of contemporary society. As a missional theology, Paul's theology of grace thus disjoined converts from their previous social and cultural presumptions, scoring a line between their past and their present, between insiders and outsiders. In Luther's context, the same theology of grace inevitably played a different role. The people he addressed had all been baptized as infants, and had been socialized, more or less successfully, in a thoroughly Christian environment. Their criteria of worth were not the central problem (in Luther's view; more radical reformers would disagree); it was rather their sense that they could and should acquire worth within the Christianized systems of value in which they were accustomed to operate. Luther's achievement was to recontextualize Paul's missionary theology into an urgent and unceasing *inward mission*, directed to the church itself and to the heart and conscience of each individual believer. What already baptized Christians needed to realize was what their baptism really meant: that God had already given them in Christ all that was necessary for salvation, to be received by faith, and that the works that resulted from this faith were never instrumental in acquiring some further or final grace from God. Where Paul spoke of works of the law in the sense of the observance of the Jewish Torah, Luther (following Augustine) read 'works' in general – in fact, good, holy works in particular. Paul's theology of grace that grounded his cross-cultural mission is thus re-used by Luther to release Christians from the burden of their misconception of the value of the Christian good works that they performed.

This inward mission is for Luther a perpetual, in fact a daily, affair, because the Christian in this life lives permanently on the edge between faith and unbelief, between God and the Devil, Spirit and flesh, between power and weakness – in the permanent incongruity of *simul justus et peccator*. Thus the gospel needs to be continually re-heard, since we are constantly drawn back into relying on ourselves, rather than living in total dependence on the grace of God. Once again, there is something brilliantly insightful here, in Luther's reading of Paul, but also a decisive move that reactivates Paul's theology in a different mode. As is well known, Paul understands the Christ-event as the breaking-in of the new creation, the resurrection being the start of the new age; its powers are released by the Spirit to believers who are nonetheless still mortal, tempted, and weak, living by faith under the conditions of what Paul calls 'the present evil age' (Galatians 1.4). This is the phenomenon known in shorthand as 'already but not yet' or 'the overlap of the ages', an anomalous situation which Paul did not expect to last long, but which subsequent Christian interpreters needed to make sense of as the centuries passed. Luther entered into Paul's dialectic far more deeply than most, and he took it to represent an existential paradox fundamental to the Christian life. God's incongruous grace in Christ is here not a one-off phenomenon at the start of the Christian life, but its permanent hallmark, since, in themselves, believers remain nothing but sinful, weak, and helpless; their *only* righteousness is the righteousness of Christ, which remains in a deep sense 'not their own', even while they draw from its benefits.

What Luther tries to preserve here is the sense in Paul that the believer never 'grows out of' dependence on the grace of God: if Paul works harder than the other apostles, he insists that this is 'not I, but the grace of God that is with me' (1 Corinthians 15.10). Luther also preserves the Pauline motif of participation in Christ (or, in Morna Hooker's terms, 'interchange'), and the sense that the believer lives only out of the resurrection life of Christ: 'it is no longer I who live, but Christ who lives in me' (Galatians 2.20). This 'not us, but

God' structure is, indeed, foundational to the grammar of Christian existence, according to Paul, but the question is whether Luther gives enough weight to the accompanying grammar of human agency and believer-virtue, the grammar of 'I worked harder' and 'the life I now live' – in other words, the believer's formation, as a redeemed agent, in the holiness and God-likeness of the Spirit-led life. Luther's interpretation of Paul on this matter was strongly influenced by his reading of Romans 7 (following the later Augustine) as one side of *Christian* experience – a reading still advocated by some Pauline scholars, but now very much a minority opinion.[40] More generally, Paul's language of holiness, progress, obedience, 'walking worthily of God' (1 Thessalonians 2.12), and (ultimately) judgment by works, is difficult for a Lutheran reading of Paul to assimilate, and is one of the places where Calvin tried to repair what he felt was a weakness in Luther's theology. Luther is right that to live by faith is to live out of a newly created reality which is perpetually sourced in the grace of God. But he was less clear about how the believer is thereby rendered active, responsible, and *transformed* by participation in Christ – never perfect, to be sure, but something other than simply a *peccator* in moral terms.[41]

A parallel one-sidedness is evident, I believe, in Luther's theology of human gift-giving, with its emphasis on gift and its ambivalent, or negative, valuation of receipt. Luther is entirely right in tracing all human giving to the antecedent and enabling gift of God. Luther's images of flow, cascade, or conduit, in which God's giving in Christ passes on through the believer into generous giving to others matches the theology of 2 Corinthians 8–9 very well, where the *charis* of Christ is not just the example but the source of the human *charis* that Paul expects the Corinthians to pass on to the church in Jerusalem. That flow of generosity is exactly what Paul has in mind in the famous statement of 2 Corinthians 8.9, which I would translate, 'you know the grace of our Lord Jesus Christ, that *because* he was rich (that is, rich in self-giving love) he became poor, so that through his poverty you might become rich (that is, in generosity)'.[42]

An important characteristic of this flow is what we might call the first rule of gift-giving in Pauline ethics, which may be expressed in a 'not, but' grammar: love seeks not its own good, but the good of the other. This insistence that giving, and the love expressed in it, is always other-directed, concerned for the other's benefit, non-manipulative, and even requiring some strategic 'forgetting' of the self, is central to Paul's ethic, as Luther grasped very well. Many of his comments we noted earlier about love not seeking 'its own' (or its own good) are derived from 1 Corinthians 13.5, where Paul speaks of love 'not seeking its own' or from 1 Corinthians 10.24 where he instructs, 'let no-one seek his own good but the good of the other' (cf. 1 Corinthians 10.33, applied to himself). Similarly, when speaking of being 'Christs' to our neighbours, Luther frequently refers to Romans 15.2–3 ('let each person please his neighbour, for his good and upbuilding, for Christ did not please himself') and Philippians 2, where the Christ-hymn about the one who emptied himself and took the form of a servant (2.6–11) is preceded by the instruction, 'let each look not to their own interests, but to the interests of others' (2.4).[43] Luther is right that this 'not for myself, but for the other' is a basic rule of the gift in Pauline, and thus in Christian, giving, and that Paul gives this a strong Christological warrant.

However, what Luther seems less disposed to recognize is that there are other complementary (not contradictory) rules of giving in Paul, which seem equally necessary. If the first rule is, as we have said, 'not for me, but for you', the second we may summarize as 'both for you and for me', in the sense that this gift-giving is intended to create not unilateral but reciprocal patterns of interdependence in which I am intended to be both giver and receiver. To be fair, Luther does presume this interdependence when he speaks of life together in family and society;[44] he also echoes Paul's language of 'bearing one another's burdens' (Galatians 6.2), and sometimes spells this out very expressly in reciprocal terms. In a sermon of 1525, he speaks in typically vivid language of becoming one cake or loaf, and 'eating' each other. So, 'when I help and serve you in all your need, I am also your bread. Moreover, if you are also a Christ, then you, in turn, do the same thing to me: you serve me with everything you have, so that it all works for my good, and I can use it like food or drink'.[45] What I think is under-developed in Luther is the sense that this mutual interdependence in gift-giving *and gift-receiving* is structurally a part of what it means in Paul to live from grace: believers are not, and are not intended to be, the self-sufficient servants of others, but to receive as well as to give, taking part in the cascade of grace in *both* roles.

The fullest demonstration of this principle of reciprocity, and of its social ramifications, is the Pauline metaphor of the body (1 Corinthians 12.12–26; Romans 12.3–8), texts which play less part in Luther's discourse on gift than one might expect. Here the members of the body are explicitly described as united in mutual contribution. The gifts of the Spirit (*charismata*) are distributed around the body, to individual members, so that no part can say that it is self-sufficient, and none can be dispensed with, or disparaged as superfluous. 'The eye cannot say to the hand, "I have no need of you", nor can the head say to the feet, "I have no need of you"' (1 Corinthians 12.21). 'Need' is a strong word: it indicates vulnerability, exposure, the necessity to receive. Thus all the parts of the body are bound together both in gift and in need. The gift-and-return here may not be bilateral: there are more than two parts to the body, so gifts will circulate around the body in both direct and indirect forms of reciprocity. Thus what I give may not be matched by a return gift from the recipient but by a return from elsewhere in the community: as gifts circulate among us, everyone is constantly in the process of both giving and receiving.

Crucially, this reciprocity is fuelled and maintained by the fact that all parties are recipients of the Spirit's gifts – what they pass on to others is what they themselves have received. Thus the reciprocity between givers and receivers – in which each party is both (at one time, or in one respect) a giver *and* a receiver – is not just a pragmatic arrangement or a political device. It is a means of entering into the generosity and self-giving love of God. Note that we enter this not only when we give (flowing in the momentum of gift that is at the heart of God) but also when we receive, because what we receive is that same momentum as it comes to us through others. Paul's image of the body suggests that we are designed both to give and to receive, and the same is true for everyone else with whom we are in a relationship. They too are designed to enjoy the dignity and the privilege of being givers, and if we decline their gift, or refuse their return, we are denying them the opportunity of entering into the momentum of grace as fully as we are claiming for ourselves. In other words, the one-way gift can be bad for the recipients of such gifts not only because they may be psychologically humiliated or socially demeaned, but because they end up spiritually crippled. If we refuse to accept a return, we are denying others the means by which they become rich *in giving to us*!

To put things this way may seem, to Lutheran sensibilities, suspiciously like promoting reciprocity as a mask for self-interest! In fact, however, Paul encourages the Philippians in their giving to him in something like these terms, assuring them that their gift to him is really a gift to God ('a sacrifice acceptable and pleasing to God') and that 'my God will fully satisfy every need of yours according to his riches in glory in Christ Jesus' (Philippians 4.18–19). Through their gift to him they are themselves enriched! And this reveals what we might call the third rule of Pauline gift-giving, which encompasses and unites the first two, which might otherwise appear to contradict one another. If the first rule is 'not for me, but for you' and the second 'both for you and for me', the third is that 'our benefits are neither divided nor competitive'. Transcending the 'you' and 'me' is the 'we' of our relationship with one another, a relationship in which we participate *to mutual benefit* in our giving to one another. In giving to another, I am creating a relationship of friendship (or more), in which my interests cannot be divided from theirs, nor theirs from mine: what I give is not for myself (in the sense that my benefit could be, and will be, determined *over against* theirs), but neither is it simply to my detriment, since the relationship created is designed to be mutually beneficial. The marriage metaphor that Luther uses so much could illustrate this well, because here the gifts and obligations that tie the parties together in love are not partitive or competitive. When I give to my wife, for her benefit, not mine, I am also investing in our relationship: she will not flourish without my flourishing, and I will not flourish without hers. Here, then, we could break away from the polarization of 'self-interest' and 'disinterest', and explore the language and conceptuality of 'co-interest' and participation, in which benefits are neither distributed nor divided. In Pauline terms, the relationship of 'giving and receiving' that he has with the Philippians (4.13) is ultimately a mutual participation in grace (1.6). In participating in this grace, both in giving and in receiving, believers are drawn towards their ultimate benefit and fulfilment; Paul can even speak of 'gaining' Christ (Philippians 3.8). We do not have to represent this as a form of selfishness or self-seeking, and it is only the modern turn against (and misunderstanding of) eudaimonism that has created this suspicion.

Luther's reading of Paul, which is at the core of his theological legacy, is nowhere more beneficial than in his reactivation and radicalization of Paul's theology of gift. Christ as gift, unconditioned, liberating, and cascading into the gift-giving of the believer: these are all highly significant gifts from the Reformation to the Christian tradition. With the strength comes a weakness: a focus solely on the first rule of giving ('not for me, but for you') which leads to a kind of unilateral view of gift in both God's giving and ours. If we could supplement this rule with the two others I have mentioned ('both for you and for me'; and 'our benefits are neither divided nor in competition') one might have a more rounded and more participative model of giving between God and us, one in which God's giving grounds and enables our giving of ourselves to God (2 Corinthians 8.5), a form of participation in divine gift which is not about seeking our good in the sense of 'self-interest' but about finding our fulfilment in being loved by God and in returning that love to God. And this participative model might be able to accommodate and encourage reciprocity, and even the obligations of reciprocal gift, not as a contractual debt or a transactional calculation, but as a common participation in a *koinōnia* in which benefits are shared, not divided. Thus there may be some parts of the Lutheran legacy, in its contribution to modern 'no-return' altruism, which are unhelpful in their one-sidedness. The challenge is to balance them out in a way that does not overthrow, or obscure, the multiple gifts that Luther and his Lutheran successors have bequeathed to the Christian tradition.

# Notes

1   A famous early critique of the Lutheran tradition of interpretation was issued by Krister Stendahl in his essay 'Paul and the Introspective Conscience of the Weak', republished in K. Stendahl, *Paul among Jews and Gentiles* (London: SCM Press, 1077). For an overview, see S. Westerholm, *Perspectives Old and New on Paul: The 'Lutheran' Paul and his Critics* (Grand Rapids: Eerdmans, 2004).

2   In this latter respect, the decisive impetus came from E.P. Sanders, *Paul and Palestinian Judaism* (London: SCM Press, 1977). His legacy is sharpened still further in those who identify themselves with the 'radical new perspective' (or 'Paul within Judaism'); see, e.g., M.D. Nanos and M. Zetterholm (eds.), *Paul within Judaism: Restoring the First-Century Context to the Apostle* (Minneapolis: Fortress Press, 2015).

3   This is a common theme in the work of N.T. Wright, e.g. his *Paul and the Faithfulness of God* (2 vols.; London: SPCK, 2013).

4   S.C. Chester, *Reading Paul with the Reformers: Reconciling Old and New Perspectives* (Grand Rapids: Eerdmans, 2017); M. Allen and J. Linebaugh (eds.), *Reformation Readings of Paul* (Downers Grove, IL.; InterVarsity Press, 2015).

5   The theme is ubiquitous in Derrida, but see especially J. Derrida, *Given Time.* Volume 1: *Counterfeit Money* (translated by P. Kamuf; Chicago: University of Chicago Press, 1995); cf. J.-L. Marion, *Being Given: Towards a Phenomenology of Givenness* (translated by J.L. Kosky; Stanford: Stanford University Press, 1997); K. Tanner, *Economy of Grace* (Minneapolis: Fortress Press, 2005); J. Milbank, 'Can a Gift be Given? Prolegomena towards a Future Trinitarian Metaphysic', *Modern Theology* 11 (1995), 119  61. I have given a survey of some trends in the anthropology, history, and philosophy of gift in *Paul and the Gift* (Grand Rapids: Eerdmans, 2015), 11–65.

6   See, however, B.K. Holm, Gabe und Geben bei Luther: Das Verhältnis zwischen Reziprozität und reformatorischer Rechtfertigungslehre (Berlin: de Gruyter, 2006); R. Saarinen, Luther and the Gift (Tübingen: Mohr Siebeck, 2017).

7   A Brief Instruction on What to Look for in the Gospels, LW 35.120; WA 10/1.12, 7–8.

8   *Lectures on Galatians* (1535), on Galatians 2.20; *LW* 26.178; *WA* 40/1.298, 19–21.

9   *Brief Instruction, LW* 35.119; *WA* 10/1.11, 21-22.

10  S. Zahl, 'Revisiting "the Nature of Protestantism": Justification by Faith Five Hundred
    Years On,' *New Blackfriars* (forthcoming); A. Ryrie, *Protestants: The Radicals Who
    Made the Modern World* (London: William Collins, 2017).

11  See R. Schäfer, 'Melanchthon's Interpretation of Romans 5:15: His Departure
    from the Augustinian Concept of Grace Compared to Luther's,' in T.J. Wengert and
    M.P. Graham (eds.), *Philip Melanchthon and the Commentary* (Sheffield: Sheffield
    Academic Press, 1997), 79–104. See the careful analysis in Chester, *Reading Paul*,
    148–55.

12  For analysis of *Against Latomus*, see R. Skottene, *Grace and Gift: An Analysis of a
    Central Motif in Martin Luther's* Rationis Latomianae Confutatio (Frankfurt am Main:
    P. Lang, 2007).

13  *Brief Instruction, LW* 35.120; *WA* 10/1.13, 3–6.

14  *WA TR* 5.168, 35.

15  *Heidelberg Disputation*, Thesis 28, *LW* 31.57; *WA* 1.365, 2.

16  For Luther's notion of 'alien righteousness', see Chester, *Reading Paul*, 175–217.

17  For the marriage metaphor, see, e.g., *Two Kinds of Righteousness* (1518–19) and
    *Freedom of the Christian* (1520).

18  *Freedom of a Christian, LW* 31.351; *WA* 7.54, 39–55.

19  For discussion of the 'passivity' of the Christian life, see Saarinen, *Luther and the Gift*,
    242–75.

20  *Freedom of the Christian, LW* 31.367; *WA* 7.65, 36–66, 6.

21  See B. Hamm, 'Martin Luther's Theology of Pure Gift Without Reciprocation',
    *Lutheran Quarterly* 29 (2015) 125–61; R. Saarinen, *Luther and the Gift*, 226–42;
    P. Malysz, 'Exchange and Ecstasy: Luther's Eucharistic Theology in Light of Radical
    Orthodoxy's Critique of Gift and Sacrifice', *Scottish Journal of Theology* 60 (2007)
    294–308.

22  See Holm, *Gabe und Geben*; O. Bayer, *Martin Luther's Theology. A Contemporary
    Interpretation* (translated by T.H. Trapp; Grand Rapids: Eerdmans, 2003); idem, 'The
    Ethics of Gift', *Lutheran Quarterly* 24 (2010) 447–68.

23  See in outline, Barclay, *Paul and the Gift*, 24–32. For the associations of gift in the
    sixteenth century, see N. Zemon Davis, *The Gift in Sixteenth-Century France* (Oxford:
    Oxford University Press, 2000).

24  *Treatise on Good Works, LW* 44.64; *WA* 6.237, 32.

**25** *Treatise on Good Works, LW* 44.31; *WA* 6.210, 19–22.

**26** *Heidelberg Disputation,* Thesis 28, *LW* 31.57; *WA* 1.365, 2–3, 7–8, 10. For a Lutheran exposition of this antithesis, see T. Mannermaa, *Two Kinds of Love: Martin Luther's Religious World* (translated by K. Stjerna; Minneapolis: Fortress Press, 2010).

**27** *LW* 11.403; *WA* 4.269, 25–26.

**28** *Lectures on Romans, LW* 25.345; *WA* 56.356, 4–6.

**29** *Freedom of a Christian, LW* 31.368, 370; *WA* 7.66, 36–37; 7.68, 22–23.

**30** *The Magnificat, LW* 21.309; *WA* 7.556, 26.

**31** Two Kinds of Righteousness, LW 31.300; *WA* 2.147, 31–32.

**32** *Freedom of a Christian, LW* 31.364; *WA* 7.64, 15–17.

**33** *Freedom of a Christian, LW* 31.365; *WA* 7.64, 27–28.

**34** *Freedom of a Christian, LW* 31.367; *WA* 7.66, 7–12.

**35** Hamm, 'Martin Luther's Revolutionary Theology', 139.

**36** A. Nygren, *Agape and Eros* (translated by P. Watson; London: SPCK, 1982).

**37** W. Cavanaugh, 'Eucharistic Sacrifice and the Social Imagination in Early Modern Europe', *Journal of Medieval and Early Modern Studies* 31 (2001) 585–605.

**38** See Barclay, *Paul and the Gift,* 97–116. See, further, Chester, *Reading Paul with the Reformers.*

**39** Barclay, *Paul and the Gift,* 569–74.

**40** For a contemporary defence of this reading, however, see W.N. Timmins, *Romans 7 and Christian Identity: A Study of the 'I' in its Literary Context* (Cambridge: Cambridge University Press, 2017).

**41** It is sometimes charged that Luther worked with a theologically faulty notion of a competitive relationship between divine and human agency, and thus could understand God's activity as effective only if the believer is *passive.* For a different perspective, highlighting Luther's existential conviction that claims of significant, durable moral transformation were simply empirically untrue, see S. Zahl, 'Non-Competitive Agency and Luther's Experiential Argument Against Virtue', *Modern Theology* (forthcoming).

**42** For this translation, see J. M.G. Barclay, '"Because he was rich he became poor": Translation, Exegesis and Hermeneutics in the Reading of 2 Cor 8.9', in Reimund Bieringer, Ma. Marilou S. Ibita, Dominika A. Kurek-Chomycz, and Thomas A. Vollmer (eds.), *Theologizing in the Corinthian Conflict: Studies in the Exegesis and Theology of 2 Corinthians* (Leuven – Paris – Walpole MA: Peeters, 2013) 331–44.

**43** However, some, probably better, texts read 'but *also* to the interests of others', which suggests that one's own interests are not ignored.

**44** In the Large Catechism, for instance, he emphasizes the blessings we receive from parents and from rulers, as channels of God's blessing to us (e.g., on the First Commandment, 26–27; on the Fourth Commandment, 127–28; on the Lord's Prayer, 75–76; Theodore G. Tappert (ed.), *The Book of Concord: The Confessions of the Evangelical Lutheran Church* (trans. Theodore G. Tappert; Philadelphia: Fortress, 1959), 368, 382–83, 430–31.

**45** *WA* 12.489, 9–490, 5, cited in Mannermaa, *Two Kinds of Love*, 74–75.

# 2

# Luther – faithful exegete of Paul

*Morna D. Hooker*

This paper began life as a response to John Barclay's contribution to the Seminar on Luther. Beguiled into agreeing to take on the role of respondent by seeing the name 'Paul' in the title, it was only on reading his paper that I realized, too late, that it would have been far more helpful to know something about Luther than something about Paul! Whatever expertise I may have, it is not in the field of Luther's studies. I am, however, grateful to both John for making me look at Luther once again, and so allowing me to discover aspects of his teaching of which I had previously been unaware.

I encountered a second difficulty in composing my original response, however, since I found myself in almost total agreement with everything that John said, and therefore unable to take issue with him. In this happy state, the best I could do was to highlight some of his points and raise one or two possible queries. The invitation to expand what I originally said has enabled me to explore further the question of the correspondence between the teaching of Paul and that of Luther.

# Distortion?

John began by pointing to two debates which have been taking place in recent years. The first arises from the so-called 'new perspective on Paul' and concerns Luther's reliability as an interpreter of Paul. John reminded us of the recent criticism of Luther as a 'poor interpreter of Paul', and picked out Luther's 'introspective conscience', his individualism, and his reading of the faith-works antithesis, as examples of his so-called 'misconstrual' of Paul – a supposed misconstrual that has been condemned as having 'infected the whole Protestant exegetical tradition for 500 years'. Later on he discussed Luther's change in emphasis, reminding us that 'in activating [the] Pauline legacy in the context of the 16th century, Luther inevitably altered its focus in key respects'. I would like to stress that word 'inevitably'.

In recent years, as John has said, Luther has been blamed for distorting Paul's gospel. But what Luther did was to interpret it in the context of his day. Paul's gospel had been addressed to *outsiders*, and he was concerned to stress that God's grace extends to all – to Gentiles as well as to Jews. Luther was addressing *insiders* – baptized Christians, brought up in a Christian environment. His situation was more akin to that of Jesus calling his fellow-Jews back to the faith of their fathers than to that of Paul, calling Gentiles to accept what to them seemed a new religion. In other words – John's words – 'Luther's achievement was to recontextualize Paul's missionary theology into an urgent and unceasing inward mission, directed to the church itself and to the heart and conscience of each individual believer'. The situation had of course changed long before Luther – with the break between Jews and Christians in the second century. Inevitably, when Paul's words were read in the new situation, they seemed to take on new meaning – a situation where the conscience of the individual, rather than the inclusion of the Gentiles in God's people, became the focus of his argument – and this meant that by the sixteenth century, inevitably, his teaching was interpreted as implying a conflict between law and gospel, and as a condemnation of Jews and Judaism.

The criticisms regarding Luther's interpretation of Paul are brought by modern exegetes who are using historical tools in their attempts to reconstruct Paul's message for his own particular situation, and insisting, as John expressed it, that Paul must 'be viewed in his own original terms, not "through Reformation spectacles"'. Such exegetes need constantly to be reminded that they, too, bring their own presuppositions to the interpretation of the text, and that their own 'spectacles' may well be distorting Paul's meaning. But for the *Christian* exegete the historical questions are not the only ones to be answered, and Luther's attempts to interpret Paul and the criticisms levelled against him pinpoint a particular problem. For those who regard Paul's letters as scripture, there are other questions to be faced – questions concerning the meaning of the text for Christians in their own time, whether that be the sixteenth or twenty-first century. Luther himself may not have made the distinction between the meaning of the text 'then' and 'now', but it was clearly questions regarding the meaning for his own day which dictated his approach.

What Luther did was, as John neatly expressed it, to make 'a decisive move that reactivates Paul's theology in a different mode'. He cannot be blamed for doing what any good pastor should do – namely, for interpreting the message of scripture for the Church in his own time and situation – though we might perhaps blame those who followed him and who regarded his interpretation (or their understanding of it!) as though it had been written on stone, thus allowing it to dominate Protestant exegesis for the next four hundred years and more. We can surely honour Luther for re-interpreting Paul in the sixteenth century – a re-interpretation which proved so successful and world-changing – and learn from what he wrote, without necessarily assuming, as he himself did, that this interpretation was what Paul himself had meant to say, or condemning him for 'distorting' Paul's original message. Whether or not he *did* 'distort' it is a question to which we must return.

# Grace and gift

The second debate highlighted by John in his introduction concerns 'grace' and 'gift', which Luther apparently sometimes treated as though they were synonyms, but which he elsewhere distinguished. If so, he was in good company, since Paul does much the same. For both, it would seem that the grace of God is the fundamental idea, but this is focused in the gift, and for Luther this is, as John says, 'first and foremost, Christ himself' (pp. 2–3). This gift is received through faith. Christians are entirely dependent on this gift, and 'they are made righteous, good and strong not in themselves, but in Christ, that is by being joined to *his* righteousness, goodness, wisdom and strength' (p. 4). Here we notice the theme of participation in Christ, so important to Paul, to which we must return. This participation means that 'to live by faith is to live in perpetual receipt of the gift'.

Because the gift is grounded in grace, it is for both Paul and Luther distinct from what John terms the 'self-seeking systems of exchange' – i.e. the 'keeping up with the Jones' mentality – which governs much giving, both in the ancient world and today. This applies not only to our relationship with God – we cannot barter with him – but to our relationship with others, where our giving is based on the prior gift of God: 'For Luther, to be a recipient of the gift is also to be its conduit'. Instead of the circularity of giving we have a 'divine cascade of gift' – a neat way of describing the teaching of Paul – e.g. in 2 Cor. 8:9, where he sums up the relationship between God's grace and our giving by reminding the Corinthians that they 'know the grace of our Lord Jesus Christ', demonstrated in his giving-up riches in exchange for poverty for our sake. Paul then appeals to them to give to the collection he is making for the poor in Jerusalem. Because those who are 'in Christ' have experienced his grace in his self-giving, they are bound to follow his example, since it is the foundation of their existence. This, as John says, 'matches' the idea of the 'cascade of gifts' – but I would have liked to hear more from him about whether and how Luther appeals to this particular text.

According to Luther, Paul 'describes the human being as so completely turned in on himself that he not only twists bodily goods toward himself, but also spiritual goods, and seeks himself in all things'. This is applied by Luther to his contemporaries, who are concerned only with their own welfare and salvation. Our own giving 'should seek no benefit for the giver', but be concerned only for the welfare of others. Luther interpreted Paul's references to 'works of the law' in terms of 'good, holy works'. John is surely right in seeing this as a proper reinterpretation of Paul's teaching in his own situation, since 'works' were being misused in the sixteenth century, as 'works of the law' had been in Paul's time, as ways of acquiring further grace from God – in effect, as bargaining counters.

## Interchange?

John tells us (p. 13) that 'Luther... preserves the Pauline motif of participation in Christ (or "interchange")'. 'Interchange' is the term that I myself have used to describe the idea which I regard as the heart of Pauline teaching – the idea that Christ becomes what we are in order that, *in him*, we might become what he is.[1] Is this what Luther meant when he referred to a 'happy exchange', an idea that John referred to earlier in his paper (p. 4)? It is important to remember, first of all, that the term 'exchange' is not itself a word that implies participation. *A* can exchange places with *B*, as Sydney Carton did with Charles Darnay in *A Tale of Two Cities*, but this does not imply mutuality. Moreover, Luther uses the phrase with reference to Ephesians 5, a passage which he links with Hosea 1–2; what belongs to the bridegroom (i.e. righteousness) is exchanged with what belongs to the bride (i.e. sin). This is an exchange, but it is not participation or 'interchange', which is basically an *incarnational* model: i.e., because Christ, by becoming man, *shares* our state of sinfulness, and what that brings, we are able to share his righteousness and what *that* brings.

Other passages in Luther's writings, however, suggest that by the term 'exchange' Luther was thinking primarily of something which takes place because the believer is *in Christ*, and is therefore what many Pauline scholars today would describe as 'participation' or 'interchange'. By faith, the believer participates in the attributes of Christ – something to which John drew our attention earlier in his paper. The following passage for example, is clearly influenced by 2 Corinthians 5:21, where Paul writes of Christ being made sin, in order that, *in him*, we might become the righteousness of God:[2]

> Lord Jesus, you are my righteousness, just as I am your sin. You have taken upon yourself what is mine and have given to me what is yours. You have taken upon yourself what you were not and have given to me what I was not...

And on Gal. 3:13 Luther writes:[3]

> By this fortunate exchange (*feliciter commutans*) with us He took upon Himself our sinful person and granted us His innocent and victorious person. Clothed and dressed in this, we are freed from the curse of the law, because Christ Himself voluntarily became a curse for us.

There appears to be evidence here that Luther is closer to Paul's teaching than those who accuse him of 'distorting' it allow. In the last forty years or so – long after I myself studied Luther's teaching at University! – a new 'school' of Luther research has become established in Finland, where scholars have questioned the traditional 'Lutheran' understanding of his theology, which has emphasized the forensic understanding of Christ's death. The discussion has been led by Tuomo Mannermaa, and the debate centres on the interpretation of the Greek term dikaiosu/nh, which can be translated into English as 'righteousness' or 'justification'. Mannermaa has argued that for Luther himself, the term meant not only being 'justified', i.e. *declared* righteous – guilt-free – by God, but also being *made* righteous – holy – in personal union with God.

God's gift of Christ means that the believer becomes *a participant in what Christ is*. Although Lutheranism has emphasized the forensic interpretation of the Greek term, understanding it primarily as 'justification', Mannermaa has pointed to passages in Luther's writings which emphasize the 'effective' side of righteousness, achieved through Christ living in the believer, in other words, through 'participation' in Christ. To be 'justified' is not just to be *declared* righteous in the sight of God, but to be *made* righteous in Christ, by sharing in *his* righteousness:[4]

> It is Christ who forms and fulfills faith, or who is the form of faith. Therefore the Christ who is grasped by faith and who lives in the heart is the true Christian righteousness, on account of which God counts us righteous.

As we have seen, the phrase 'happy exchange' is one way in which Luther describes this gift in Christ, but Mannermaa suggests that a more accurate expression of Luther's meaning is found in another phrase which he uses, namely 'communication of attributes' (*communicatio idiomatum*).[5] Mannermaa has even argued that this implies *theosis*, or divinization.[6] Certainly in a sermon on the letter to the Ephesians, Luther (referring to 2 Peter 1) declares 'that we are to become participants in the divine nature and ... have Him, the Lord Himself, dwelling in us in His fullness'.[7] Mannermaa argues that 'the idea of the divine life in Christ that is present in faith lies at the very center of the theology of the Reformer'.[8] Christ is not so much the object of faith as 'the one who is present *in* the faith'.[9] Both this statement and the slogan *Christus forma fidei*[10] – Christ the form of faith – sound remarkably close to the interpretation of Paul's use of the phrase pistiv Xristou= as meaning primarily the faith *of* Christ rather than faith *in* Christ which has become popular in recent years.[11] Luther himself seems to affirm both views when he writes:[12] 'This is the true faith of Christ and in Christ, through which we become members of his body.'

To those of us who are primarily Pauline scholars, Mannermaa's approach is clearly of great interest, especially since those who have taken part in the so-called 'New Look' at Paul have tended to blame Luther for the emphasis on justification as a forensic transaction which has dominated Protestant interpretation of Paul ever since the Reformation. Those of us who have insisted that the centre of Paul's theology is to be found in the notion of 'participation', which comes about through 'interchange in Christ', are now told that Luther, too, understood the importance of this concept for Paul, and that it is 'Lutheranism', not Luther, that is responsible for distorting Paul's teaching. Just as 'Paulinism', attempting to apply Paul's teaching to a later age, is by no means the same as Paul's own theology, so it is with 'Lutheranism' and Luther. The irony is that in both cases, what each writer was *thought* to have said was turned into doctrine which was expected to be accepted by later generations, and that teaching which had been applied to particular situations was assumed to be the interpretation that was valid for all time.

But is the understanding of Luther's interpretation of Paul brought to us by Finnish scholars correct? Taking down a much-underlined copy of a book which I certainly studied in my undergraduate days,[13] I found that they were not the first to notice these aspects of Luther's theology, though these have frequently been ignored. When I turned to Luther's own writings, I found that many of the passages to which the Finnish scholars appeal appear to support their view. In 1 Cor. 1:30, for example, Paul reminds the Corinthians that they are 'in Christ Jesus, who has become our wisdom, and righteousness, and holiness, and redemption', an idea which is echoed by Luther in his *Sermo de duplici iustitiae* (1518):[14]

> Through faith in Christ, therefore, Christ's righteousness becomes our righteousness and all that he has becomes ours; rather, he himself becomes ours. ... He who trusts in Christ exists in Christ; he is one with Christ, having the same righteousness as he.

The same passage from 1 Corinthians – linked with Johannine vocabulary – is echoed in another sermon, preached as early as 1514:[15]

Just as the word of God became flesh, so it is certainly also necessary that the flesh may become word. In other words: God becomes man so that man may become God. Thus power becomes powerless so that weakness may become powerful. The Logos puts on our form and pattern, our image and likeness, so that it may clothe us with its image, its pattern, and its likeness. Thus wisdom becomes foolish so that foolishness may become wisdom, and so it is in all other things that are in God and in us, to the extent that in all these things he takes what is ours to himself in order to impart what is his to us.

This is true 'interchange', not 'exchange', since, as Luther goes on to say, God does not stop being God, and man does not stop being man. Significantly, Luther's words here echo the idea expressed by 'aeus, which so brilliantly sums up Paul's theology – 'Christ was made what we are, in order that he might make us what he is.'[16] Christ and humanity do not *exchange* places; rather, because Christ becomes man, men and women are enabled, *through union with him*, to become what Christ is. So, in his Commentary on Galatians, he writes:[17]

He became Law to the Law, sin to sin, and death to death, in order that He might redeem me from the curse of the Law, justify me, and make me alive. And so Christ is both: while he is the Law, he is liberty; while he is sin, he is righteousness, and while he is death, he is life. For by the very fact that he permitted the Law to accuse him, sin to damn him, and death to devour him he abrogated the Law, damned sin, destroyed death, and justified and saved me.

For Paul, this experience meant that it was no longer he who lived, but Christ who lived in him (Gal.2:20), and in his lectures on Galatians Luther echoes Paul's words, significantly using the word *manet*, 'remains': 'Christ remains in me, and that life lives in me, and the life through which I live is Christ.'[18] The gift is an ongoing one. We may compare John Barclay's comment that Luther preserves Paul's sense 'that the believer never "grows out of" dependence on the grace of God' (p. 13). Furthermore, Luther argues that Christians bear the name 'Christians' precisely 'because he dwells in us, that is, because we believe in him and are Christs one to another and do to our neighbors as Christ does to us'.[19] What this means is well-described by John as 'a cascade of gifts'.

In the teaching of Paul, the idea of 'interchange' brings together the doctrines of 'incarnation' and 'atonement'. It is because Christ was born as a man that he was able to overcome sin. Luther took seriously Paul's statements in Gal. 3:13 that Christ was 'made a curse' and in 2 Cor. 5:21 that 'Christ became sin', maintaining – in words as shocking as Paul's – that Christ was 'the greatest sinner'.[20] In his lectures on Galatians 3:13 he writes:[21]

All the prophets saw this, that Christ was to become the greatest thief, murderer, adulterer, robber, desecrator, blasphemer, etc., there has ever been anywhere in the world. . . . He is a sinner, who has and bears . . . . all the sins of all men in his body. . . . Christ was not only found among sinners, but of His own free will and by the will of the Father He wanted to be the associate of sinners, having assumed the flesh and blood of those who were sinners and thieves and who were immersed in all sorts of sin. Therefore when the Law found Him among thieves, it condemned and executed Him as a thief.

A little later he writes:[22]

With gratitude and with a sure confidence, therefore, let us accept this doctrine, so sweet and so filled with comfort, which teaches that Christ became a curse for us, that is, a sinner worthy of the wrath of God; that He clothed Himself in our person, laid our sins upon His own shoulders, and said: 'I have committed the sins that all men have committed.' Therefore He truly became accursed according to the Law, not for Himself but, as Paul says . . . .

By this fortunate exchange with us He took upon Himself our sinful person and granted us His innocent and victorious Person. Clothed and dressed in this, we are freed from the curse of the Law, because Christ Himself voluntarily became a curse for us, saying: 'For My own Person of humanity and divinity I am blessed, and I am in need of nothing whatever. But I shall empty Myself (Phil. 2:7); I shall assume your clothing and mask; and in this I shall walk about and suffer death, in order to set you free from death'.

Earlier in his lectures on Galatians we find Luther insisting that justification depends on participation:[23]

It is unprecedented and insolent to say: 'I live, I do not live; I am dead, I am not dead; I am a sinner, I am not a sinner; I have the Law, I do not have the Law.' But this phraseology is true of Christ and through Christ. When it comes to justification, therefore, if you divide Christ's Person from your own, you are in the Law; you remain in it and live in yourself, which means that you are dead in the sight of God and damned by the Law . . . .

The same passage goes on to show how relevant the idea of participation is to Luther's insistence on the role of 'faith' rather than 'works' in justification:[24]

But faith must be taught correctly, namely, that by it you are so cemented to Christ that He and you are as one person, which cannot be separated but remains attached to Him forever and declares: 'I am as Christ'. And Christ, in turn, says: 'I am that sinner who is attached to Me, and I to him. For by faith we are joined together into one flesh and one bone.' Thus Eph. 5:30 says: 'We are members of the body of Christ, of His flesh and of His bones,' in such a way that this faith couples Christ and me more intimately than a husband is coupled to his wife. Therefore this faith is no idle quality; but it is a thing of such magnitude that it obscures and completely removes those foolish dreams of the sophists' doctrine – the fiction of a 'formed faith' and of love, of merits, our worthiness, our quality, etc.

Significantly, Luther notes that the Christian is 'joined' to Christ 'more intimately than a husband is coupled to his wife'. It would seem that he recognizes here that the marital image is insufficient to convey an attachment which he describes as being 'cemented to Christ'. What he is describing is 'participation', or 'interchange', which comes about through Christ becoming what we are.

# 'Rules' of Giving

Throughout this response to John's paper I have found myself in general agreement with it, and have wished only to underline certain aspects of what he has said. In his final section, however, he sets out three 'rules' of giving in Paul, with which I find myself in disagreement (pp.14–18). The three 'rules' he attributes to Paul are: 'not for myself but for you', 'both for you and for me', and 'our benefits are mutual', and he criticizes Luther for stressing the gift-giving rather than the gift-receiving. If it is true that Luther tends to underplay the second 'rule', then I am not really surprised! For I venture to suggest that a reading of Paul himself gives the impression that it is the *giving* that is the 'Christ-like' action. As an example, we may take the verse we referred to earlier, 2 Cor. 8:9: if Christ gave up riches for our sake, those of us who are better off must certainly help fellow-Christians who are in need. Nor is this surprising, for Paul's theology stresses the grace of God in giving – and we can only *receive* his gifts, not attempt to return them; moreover, Paul's teaching is conveyed to us in letters to converts which inevitably stress what he has given to them (the Gospel), rather than what they have given to him. Indeed, for whatever reason, Paul emphasizes his independence, and his *refusal* to be dependent on others.

The one exception is Philippians, in which Paul acknowledges what he owes to this particular church, and how they and he are mutual participants in grace (1:6). It is, then, all the more remarkable that, as John points out, in a sermon delivered in 1525 Luther writes:[25]

> When I help and serve you in all your need, I am also your bread. Moreover, if you are also in Christ, then you, in turn, do the same thing to me: you serve me with everything you have, so that it all works out for my good, and I can use it like food or drink.

This, as John admits, is an example of his *second* rule: the giving is mutual. The same idea is expressed in the very similar passage noted above, where Luther speaks of Christians being 'Christs one to another'.[26]

This idea of mutuality is certainly found in Paul, and we can find an example in the opening verses of Romans. Here Paul tactfully introduces himself to a congregation he does not know by expressing his hope that he will be able to share some spiritual gift with them, and then hastily adds that this of course means that they will be mutually encouraged by each other's faith (Rom. 1:11f.). The idea is inherent, too, in the image of the body, which John refers to as an example of his second rule, since Paul employs it in 1 Corinthians 12 because he wishes his readers to understand that the gifts exercised by each individual are intended to benefit the whole community. But Paul's reason for stressing this and for employing the image is that he has heard that the Corinthians are boasting in the gifts they have individually received, and so seeing themselves as superior to their fellow-Christians.[27] Paul's aim is to remind his converts that the spiritual gifts they enjoy are not intended for themselves alone, but in order to help others – an idea which must surely be classified as 'not for myself but for others': once again we have a 'cascade' principle – 'this gift is not for my glory, but for the benefit of others'. It can also be classified as an example of John's *third* rule, since the lesson conveyed in it is clearly that 'our benefits are neither divided nor in competition' (p. 17)!

I am not denying, then, that John's second and third rules are present in Paul – just that they are not so obvious, and that they are not so clearly different from one another, as John's categorization might suggest. Luther may be forgiven for stressing the first rule – and stressing it for the same reason that Paul himself does: that God's grace is expressed in giving, and that those who have experienced his gift must, in turn, act as conduits of that gift to others. It would seem that Luther is closer to the Pauline emphases at this point than John suggests.

## A faithful Exegete?

And so we return to the question raised at the beginning of this paper: is Luther guilty of distorting Paul's teaching, as some Pauline scholars have argued? Some things he undoubtedly got wrong: Luther's attitude to Jews, for example, which today seems so reprehensible – and once again reflects the attitudes of his own day – is a long way from that of Paul, who expressed himself willing to be cut off from Christ for the sake of his fellow-countrymen.[28] Regarding his understanding of righteousness (or justification) however, for which he has recently been pilloried, it would seem that the emphasis on 'forensic justice' and on 'works' which has characterized so much Lutheran teaching is precisely that – an emphasis on one part of Luther's teaching – of particular relevance to the concerns of certain expositors – at the expense of other aspects of his thinking. Here, we find that the 'real' Luther is much closer to Paul than we might have supposed. The contribution of Mannermaa and his colleagues in rediscovering neglected parts of Luther's teaching supports and extends John's emphasis on the importance of grace for Luther (as for Paul), and the significance of God's gift of Christ, *in whom* believers are made righteous through sharing in his righteousness, and *in whom* they *continue* to live and to grow. Whether or not we describe this as 'deification,'[29] the idea that, in Christ, we share his righteousness and become like him is Pauline to the core, and was clearly central to Luther who, like Paul, saw Incarnation and Atonement as inseparably joined: for them both, this whole idea can be summed up in Irenaeus' affirmation that Christ became what we are, in order that, in him, we might be made what he is. The grace of God is seen in the gift of Christ, who – sharing *our* human nature – shares *his* righteousness with believers and transforms them into his own likeness.

# Notes

1   See essays reprinted in Morna D. Hooker, *From Adam to Christ: Essays on Paul*, Cambridge CUP, 1990, reprinted Wipf and Stock), 2008, pp. 1–69.

2   Letter to George Spenlein, 1516, *LW* 48, p.11.

3   *LW* 26:284, WA 40/1:443, 23–6.

4   *Lectures on Galatians, LW* 26:130, WA 40/1:229, 27–30.

5   Tuomo Mannermaa, *Christ Present in Faith: Luther's View of Justification*, ed. Kirsi Stjerna, Minneapolis, MN: Fortress, 2005, p. 21.

6   See *Christ Present in Faith* throughout.

7   *Predigt* (1525) WA 17/1:438, 14–28.

8   *Christ Present in Faith*, p.5.

9   *Sic ut Christus sit objectum fidei, imo non obiectum, sed, ut ita dicam, in ipsa fide Christus adest. Commentary on Galatians, LW* 26:129; WA: 40/1:228, 34–229, 15.

10  *Lectures on Galatians, LW* 26:130; WA: 40/1:229, 9.

11  There is a vast amount of literature on this topic. See Richard B. Hays *The Faith of Jesus Christ: An Investigation of the Narrative Substructure of Galatians 3:1–4:11*, SBL Dissertation Series 56 (Chico, CA: Scholars Press, 1983; 2nd. edn. Grand Rapids, MI/ Cambridge, UK Eerdmans, 2001), for a classic statement of the theory, and M. D. Hooker, 'Another look at πίστις Χριστοῦ', *Scottish Journal of Theology*, 69, 2016, pp. 46–62 for a summary of its history.

12  *Commentary on Galatians, LW* 26:357. *Ea est vera fides Christi et in Christum, per quam membra fimus corporis eius.* WA 40/1:546, 21f.

13  Philip S. Watson, *Let God be God*, London: Epworth, 1947, pp. 102–89.

**14** *Two Kinds of Righteousness.* See *Martin Luther: Selections from His Writings*, ed. John Dillenberger, New York: Anchor Books, 1962, p.87f.

**15** *In Natali Christi*, WA 1, 28, 25–32. Although this sermon was written before 1517, its ideas are echoed in Luther's later writings.

**16** Haer. V, praef.

**17** *LW* 26:163; WA 40/1, 278, 22–8.

**18** WA 40/I, 283, 7–9: *Christus manet in me et ista vita vivit in me, et vita qua vivo, est Christus.*

**19** *The Freedom of A Christian*, *LW* 31, 368.

**20** *Commentary* on Psalm 22:1.

**21** *LW* 26:277f.; WA 40/1:433–4.

**22** *LW* 26:283f.; WA 40/1:442–3.

**23** *LW* 26:168; WA 40/1:285, 12–17.

**24** *Lectures on Galatians* (1535), *LW* 26:168–9; WA 40/1:285, 24–286, 20.

**25** WA 40/2.72,14-28. (T. Mannermaa, Two Kinds of Love, 74f.)

**26** See above, p. 6 and note 16.

**27** The same concern leads Paul to use the image of the body in Romans 12, where he urges the Romans not to think more highly of themselves than they ought to.

**28** Rom. 9:3.

**29** The terms 'deification' and 'theosis' have been used of Paul's own teaching by Michael J. Gorman, e.g. in his *Inhabiting the Cruciform God: Kenosis, Justification, and Theosis in Paul's Narrative Soteriology*, Grand Rapids MI: 2009.

# 3

# Dante, Luther and the Church

*Robin Kirkpatrick*

The most important issue here concerns the Church, the significance and even glory of the Church but also the corruption that can occur when it falls into the wrong hands. By 'the wrong hands' I mean, primarily, those of the late medieval popes. And something of how Dante may enter this crucial debate can be illustrated by the words of John Foxe in his *Ecclesiastical History* of 1570, otherwise known as the *Book of Martyrs*. Two hundred and fifty years after the poet's death, writing in the still-agonising turbulence of Tudor church-politics, Foxe can still identify quite accurately some of the essential features of Dante's thinking. Placing Dante's name alongside those of Ockham and Duns Scotus, Foxe not only recognizes that Dante too regarded the papacy as the Whore of Babylon but also indicates Dante's unwavering support for the principle of Imperial rule:

> [*Dantes a foe to the enemies of truth*]
> Dantes an Italian writer a Florentine lived in the time of Ludovicus the emperour, about the year of our Lord 1300 and took part with Marsilius Patavinus against three sorts of men, which he said were enemies to the

truth; That is, the Pope: Secondly, the order of religious men, which count them selves the children of the church, when they are children of the devil, their father: Thirdly the Doctors of decrees and decretals. Certain of his writings be extant abroad, wherein he proveth the pope not to be above the Emperour, nor to have any right or jurisdiction in the empire. He refuteth the Donation of Constantine to be a forged and feigned thing, as which neither did stand with any law or right. For the which he was taken for an heretic ... The Pope, sayeth he, of a pastor is made a wolf ... to procure with his Clergy not the word of God to be preached but his own decrees. In his canticle of purgatory, he declareth the Pope to be the whore of Babylon.[1]

Now it seems that Foxe knew Dante's work pretty well and in particular has read his political treatise, *De Monarchia*, where the argument is that the Holy Roman Emperor draws his authority directly from God, without any need for papal sanction. But to trace in more detail the view that Dante takes of both Empire and, concomitantly of the Church, we need first to wind back in historical terms to the year 1300 and then go on to look at how, poetically, his position develops in the course of the *Commedia*.

Dante sets his poem in the year 1300. And he is not alone in seeing this year as something of a turning point in European history. John Milbank, for instance, writes:

Around [the year 1300] there started to be a far greater gap between specialists and non-specialists in all fields: administration became more technical and distant ... [T]he traditional centrality in theology of participation, deification, apophaticism, allegory and the vision of the Church, as something engendered by the Eucharist all were abruptly challenged, in a fashion that proved epochally successful.[2]

Milbank here displays an antipathy which he shares with Dante – and also John Foxe – towards the administrative structures of the institutional Church.

Dante detests canon lawyers. And later we shall see that Milbank is also at one with Dante – though maybe not Foxe – in his understanding of the alternatives to ecclesial managerialism. But these alternatives are largely articulated in the poetry of the *Commedia*. And though, as Milbank observes, the year 1300 witnessed a growing fragmentation in intellectual and academic disciplines, Dante himself is not immune to this development. In response to the crisis of that year he began to develop a response that technically and professionally did lie within the sphere of political thinking that Milbank might well consider technical and professional. I shall argue later that in the poetry of the *Commedia* Dante develops an ecclesiology that may be seen, in Milbank's terms, as fully 'participatory' and sacramental. But let us begin, roughly, where Foxe suggests we should, with the *De Monarchia*, a work which is written, professionally, in scholastic Latin.

If 1300 is the year in which Dante locates his fictional journey through the otherworld, it is also a year immediately preceding Dante's exile. Forces had been gathering in Florence – Dante's native city – which were to explode under the impact of external events, involving French political ambitions and the connivance of the Roman Church. In 1301 a *coup d'etat* occurred in which Dante's party, in which he had played a leading role, was driven out. Dante himself was exiled and never returned to Florence.

In retrospect, Dante was to trace the cause of this disaster to, above all else, *Cupidigia*. It is all too easy to translate this word as Greed or Avarice. In fact it would be better to think of it as proto-capitalism. In the second half of the thirteenth century the banking industry in Florence had grown to international proportions; and its success in this respect was, for good or ill, to provide the fertiliser for Florentine Renaissance culture. But Dante would not have been impressed by the Renaissance. As the banks flourished so did the city, growing in size and population. But this growth itself challenged, throughout Italy, the order that hitherto had been represented by the Holy Roman Empire. Simultaneously, the Church, benefitting from a very slick bureaucratic operation, began to seek territorial advancement, often striking up advantageous alliances with the banking houses of the city republics.

From the early years of his exile Dante had been developing, speculatively, the remedy that he was to pursue even when he was writing the early cantos of the *Paradiso*. His hope was that The Empire would reassert itself and, in exercising justice, restore the fortunes of the poet, unjustly exiled. This hope proved wholly unrealistic. But in philosophical terms the *Monarchia* embodies some of the most essential principles of Dante's thinking. Specifically, the Empire – even in its ancient Roman form – was for Dante directly appointed by God as ruler of the whole of humanity, and in that aspect was commissioned to control and repress the *cupidigia* or rampant greed that infected both secular and ecclesial society. In the opening chapter of this book Dante proclaims that where there is any speck of Greed there can be no justice – since all things are thrown out of proportion, by this single impurity. Imperial justice in extirpating any such contamination can, Dante believes, lead us to perfect happiness in this temporal life. Properly the Church was intended to lead us to happiness in the eternal life. So idiosyncratically Dante insists that human beings were created to enjoy two forms of beatitude, one eternal and one temporal. But the mercantile life and the behaviour of the Church in its contemporary manifestation threaten to deprive us of both.

Now one of the functions of the Empire was to maintain the Church in the state of poverty that ensured a proper direction towards the other world. There were others who, like Dante, saw the need for this, notably the Franciscans. But of course none met with any great success – otherwise there would have been no Medici popes for Luther to rail against. Nor, to remain in the year 1300, would Dante have had Pope Boniface VIII as his *bête noire* – his *bête noire par excellence*. Boniface had risen to the papacy – under rather suspicious circumstances – in 1294. He was a canon lawyer who immediately set about asserting the universal dominion of the Church, as a result becoming deeply implicated in the power struggles that resulted as new nation states, especially France, developed in the vacuum left by a declining Empire.

Now unrepeatable things were said about Boniface by his contemporaries. And Dante is not slow to join the chorus. But he does so with as much subtlety as satirical edge. And there are complications here – which are registered above all in Dante's poetry. These are focused around the fact that in 1330 Boniface declared a Jubilee year – the first Roman jubilee. Crowds of pilgrims flocked to Rome, enriching the city considerably. That may well have been Boniface's prime intention, to swell otherwise depleted coffers. The project was a success. The rebuilding of St Peter's was one consequence. Another was the development of that same sale of indulgences which was to stir Luther's justified wrath. For all that, Dante in setting his own poem in the Jubilee year, seems to still allow the efficacy of a jubilee even when promulgated by a monstrous perversion of all that a pope should ever be. In the opening cantos of the *Purgatorio* he meets those who have benefitted from, so to speak, a fast track to salvation and the whole of that *cantica* is supported by the notion that prayers for the dead and with the dead is a central Christian practice.

Now I don't really know (but would be glad to be told) what use Luther has for Purgatory or for prayers to the dead. But for Dante this is a central feature of the Purgatory. This is the most original part of the Commedia. And I shall return in conclusion to one canto which deals with confession and the remission of sins.

But the theme we are pursuing is no less prominent in the *Inferno* and *Paradiso* and I want now to turn to these outer *cantiche*, beginning with the extraordinarily complex and also vicious consideration of papacy, Church and indeed his own fate that is to be found in *Inferno* Canto 19.

This canto directly talks about corruption in the papal office. Or else to use the medieval term, simony – according to Simon Magus from the Book of Acts, 8:9–24.

You! Magic Simon and your sorry school!

Things that are God's own – things that, truly, are

the brides of goodness – lusting cruelly

 after gold and silver, you turn them all to whores.

*Inferno* 19: 1–4

The simonists are placed in one of the lower divisions of Hell where various forms of deceit are punished; and though this is the one canto in the *Inferno* that deals with specifically ecclesiastical sin, it is also the canto in which reference is made most explicitly to the Christian scriptures. Thus the opening *terzina* – as well as invoking the Acts of the Apostles – contains in lines 1 to 6 a reference, which would have drawn the attention of the protestant John Foxe, to the Whore of Babylon, as also more explicitly in lines 106 to 111, which refers directly to The Book of Revelation.

Saint John took heed of shepherds such as you.

He saw revealed that She-above the Waters

whoring it up with rulers of the world.

*Inferno* 19: 100–3

Things in the created world that are sacred, or sacramentally, dedicated (or indeed *married*) to human beings are desecrated by papal cupidity and worshipped idolatrously in their own right. Nor does Dante fail – any more than Foxe will fail later – to trace such perversions (at lines 115 to 117) to the Donation of Constantine, in which The Emperor's apparent generosity first kindled in the Church an appetite for temporal possessions.

But how is Dante in this assault to ensure that Boniface VIII is the immediate target of his polemic. There seems to be a problem here, since in the year 1300 – when the poem is set – Boniface is, inconveniently, not yet dead and so cannot plausibly be depicted in Hell. There were many, of course, who had already begun to slam the pope. But Dante, in negotiating the demands of his fictive dating, avoids the virulent name calling that characterized the writings of his contemporaries, and produces an episode which is one of the most satirical, even comical in the whole *Commedia* and also in theological terms one of the most incisive and significant.

Following Dante's rather fiendish imagination, one notes firstly how precisely he has calculated the punishment allocated to the corrupt popes: All those who through history qualify as such are plunged one above the other head down in an infernal well. So the most recent pope to arrive here after death – in this case Pope Nicholas III who died in 1280 – is encountered with his feet still protruding from the open rim of the well. Clearly, Dante intends here a parody of the apostolic succession; and the parody becomes more scandalous still when he describes how the soles of the pontifical feet have been oiled and set alight; the head of a true priest might be anointed, up-turned popes find their feet oiled with flames that unmistakeably recall, in parodic form, the fires of Pentecost.

The first consequence of all this is that Dante, in his very long conversation with Pope Nicholas, is addressing a pair of wriggling and twisting feet: 'At which – all feet – the spirit thrashed about.' But it is now that Boniface makes an appearance. Or worse than that actually doesn't. Not being able to see who is addressing him, the pope assumes that the person standing by him is the next pope destined to arrive in Hell, a welcome arrival since at least it will push Nicholas down one further rung in the well and relieve his feet from the fire. And of course, though not yet dead, that pope is infamous Boniface VII. So Dante solves the historical inconvenience. But he does so in a way that involves him directly in an outrageous farcical scene.

> And he yelled: 'Is that you standing there?
> Are you there on your feet still, Boniface?'

> *Inferno* 19: 52–3

In other words Dante depicts himself being mistaken for his own most bitter enemy. He shows himself to be utterly staggered by the mistake over his identity.

But this mistake itself has a radically theological dimension. Quite explicitly and emphatically, Dante has at lines 16–8 compared the wells into which the popes are plunged into baptismal fonts, specifically the fonts that in the Florentine Baptistery are set into the floor of that great building, which is the centre of civic and religious life in Florence. Indeed he points to an episode in his own life – no one knows exactly what he is referring to – when he was accused, it seems, of rescuing a child from suffocation in one of these – and was apparently accused of damaging church property. The point here is two-fold. Simoniac popes 'adulterate' the things of the Church where Dante's action was intended to save a life. More radically still however, baptism, which should be the restoration of our name in God's sight, in this case is utterly perverted, depriving Dante of his entire identity. The very meaning of the Church in its sacramental foundation is here threatened. One might add that the Baptistery was also the place where infant Florentines had bestowed on them their civic identity.

Now against this, Dante devises a riposte which must surely be seen as an affirmation of scriptural truth. He represents himself as a true priest giving confession to the Pope now pictured as a felon condemned to death. Here again there is an element of black comedy. Dante in fact ironically describes his diatribe against the upturned pope as 'crazy'. Yet this is the longest speech that Dante gives to himself in the *Inferno*, and also the speech that bears the most explicit stamp of scriptural reference. Thus Dante here concludes with the penetratingly simple question:

> What riches did Our Lord
> > demand, as first instalment, from Saint Peter
> > before he placed the keys in his command?
> He asked (be sure) no more than 'Come behind me.'

*Inferno.*19: 90–93

And even in this staggeringly simple two-word summary of Christian mission there is comedy. This has been a canto about feet. The sins of the papal feet, in failing to follow Christ's simple command, are grotesquely and agonisingly revealed to view.

It will, perhaps, already be obvious that the scandalized – and indeed scandalous – polemic of *Inferno* 19 must itself be seen as the reverse side of Dante's profound commitment to those principles that a True church might be expected to adhere to. On this understanding, the sacraments – so viciously parodied here – must have had especial significance to the poet.

I'll hope to show something of this, in its positive aspect, when I turn to the *Purgatorio* and *Paradiso*. There is, however, a point here that needs, I think, for two reasons, to be given some emphasis.

In the first place, Dante-scholars have not always shown much interest in the ways that Christian practice may have influenced the poet's imagination. There has been a tendency to view him, especially considering his exile from his native Florence, as a lone individualist. Indeed, he himself at times invites that view. And, so far, if I have spoken of Dante's interest in the social and communal life, it has been in relation to his devotion to a vision of political justice embodied in the Empire. From now on, without retracting any of that, I shall argue for a parallel concern where Dante seeks to re-discover and live within the community of the True Church as the Body of Christ. In that community, *cupidigia* – the root of all division, social and spiritual – will be countered not only by Justice but also by love and *caritas*.

A second reason for this change of gear is that it will lead us not only to the heights of the *Paradiso* but also back to the analysis offered by John Milbank (above) and allow us to travel beyond those ecclesial hierarchies and technocracies that Milbank there identifies as emerging around the year 1300. But if 1300 is the beginning of that dreadful development, then 1500 accelerates its progress. In the Reformation – Catholic as well as Protestant – individualism joins hands with organized and militant sectarianism. And Dante's voice may be needed to call us away from that suicidal march.

So let us turn in hopes to the next passages on the hand-out, all of which come from a sequence of cantos (*Paradiso* 27 to 29) immediately preceding the final encounter with God, in *Paradiso* 33.

Canto 27 begins (lines 1–9):

> 'To Father and Son and the Holy Ghost,
> Glory on high!' all Heaven here began,
> till I, at that sweet song, reeled drunkenly.
>     And what I saw, it seemed, was now the laughter
> of the universe. So drunkenness, for me,
> came in through hearing and, no less, through sight.
>     The joy of that! The happiness beyond all words!
> A life of peace and love, entire and whole!
> Riches all free of craving, trouble-less.

The Trinitarian doxology of this opening is directly liturgical in character. But the church – so to speak – in which this hymn is sung is the universe itself, in its widest and highest expanse. (Dante has now journeyed to the outermost circles of the planetary system.) The celebrants are the whole company of the saints, including St Peter. And the tonality of this song is one not of piety but of rhythmic – even drunken – energy. The cosmic order and the human creatures within laughs aloud, and the joy of that laughter is directly contrasted with the anxiety and petty irritations that accompany our avaricious or cupidinous cravings for possessions and wealth:

But then, all of a sudden, the energies of this opening are directed back to the same target that Dante aimed at in *Inferno* 19. Where in *Inferno* 19 Dante's commitment to the Church was filtered through agonisingly comic satire, it now reveals itself with explicit and excoriating ardour. The laughter of the universe is transformed into the burning red of an apoplectic blush; and St Peter himself – the rock of the Church – turns in irrepressible indignation on his successors in the Holy See. As Peter, on Maundy Thursday, had three times denied any knowledge of Christ, now in Heaven he repeats three times his claim to the place where he himself was martyred – a place that Papal corruption has now turned into a 'shit-hole' in which Satan – the 'sod who fell from Heaven' takes a perverse delight:

> He who on earth has robbed me of my place,
>
> my place, my place – which therefore in the sight
>
> of God's dear son stands vacant now – has made
>
>    of my own burial ground a shit hole
>
> reeking of blood and pus. In this the sod
>
> who fell from here down there takes sheer delight.'
>
>    With that same colour that a cloud takes on,
>
> morning or evening, when it meets the sun,
>
> I saw in every part the Heavens flush.

*Paradiso* 27: 19–30

So even in the highest reaches of Heaven, anger and polemic have still a place in Dante's rhetorical arsenal. And I have to say that, if we were to go on to *Paradiso* 29, we should find that not only popes but also academics and scholars are treated with similarly abrasive vigour: intellectual preachers – or as Milbank might suggest the new professionals – are derided in that canto for preferring witty anecdotes and clever debating points instead of preaching the truths of the Cross, of martyrdom and sacrifice. But I want here rather to divert attention away from polemic and back to doxology, especially as displayed in *Paradiso* Canto 28 where the physical order of the cosmos is seen to be related to the supernal order of the angels in their adoration of their Creator and where, sacramentally, the whole universe may be viewed as a Church.

Canto 28 might, in a word, be seen as Dante's own version of the *Sanctus,* and so compared to that moment in the Mass where our human voices pray to be joined with those of the angels, declaring that Heaven and Earth are full of God's glory and praying to participate in the abundant life of their Creator. Let me frame the implications of this sequence by two further references to contemporary theology.

The first is, again, drawn from John Milbank's discussion of Nicholas Cusanus in *Being Reconciled* (*op cit*. pp. 126–7):

> the angels are guardians of ecclesial places. [*Cusanus*] offers perhaps one of the fullest exhibitions ever of the multiple paradoxes of hierarchy.

On this view there can be no bishops unless there are angels who correspond to them and directly – and again sacramentally – co-involve the Episcopal order with the order of Creation. And, as Dante will shortly make plain, any such involvement will involve conceptions of hierarchy very different from those that characterize the pyramidal power structures or technocracies of temporal power. Milbank's mention of 'paradox' is important here. But one might also turn here to a true bishop, Rowan Williams, in preparation for a return to Dante's text. In an essay on Balthasar, Williams quotes Balthasar's opposition to 'the hegemony of instrumental reasoning' and points himself beyond any such hegemony to the relational character of existence as established in the Trinity:

> Here we discover a two-fold negation of individual self-assertion, a refusal to be for oneself alone and a refusal to look for the ground of one's being in an individuality divorced from relation.... The work of grace makes us ourselves; but we are ourselves only in the eternal Son. The purpose, then, of a Church is to reveal to us and encourage our participation in a cosmic and Trinitarian liturgy that, so far from engaging an instrumental or bureaucratic structure, draws us directly into the pure freedom of God's creative grace.
>
> *Cambridge Companion to Hans Urs von Balthasar,*
> Cambridge 2009, pp. 41–2

In that light, it is striking that Dante describes the nine orders of angels – ranging from Seraphim down to Archangels and the modest little Angels themselves – as *playing* angelic games in the sight of God (line 126): 'angelici ludi'. That phrase already beckons us away from hierarchy in any familiar sense and away also from bureaucratic officialdom into a realm which, in its interweaving of difference modes of existence, might well be seen as choreographic. So from the very first *Paradiso* 28 calls wonderfully into question our conceptions of how the power of God is to be appreciated and offers, in the patternings of its poetry, a verbal equivalent of angelic play.

This canto begins with the first sight of God's actual dwelling place. But here at once our expectations are defeated. By any ordinary – or hierarchical – logic, God's habitation should be bigger than, greater than and far, far beyond anything that we can comprehend. Yet in fact God is here seen as an infinitesimally sharp point of light, located within, not beyond, its own creation. The angels are related to this by a further inversion of expectation: the highest orders are closest to that single point and their rank – if it can be called that – is decided not by magnitude but by proximity and intensity. There follows a further step in what Dante calls the 'miraculous logic' of this new formulation: this 'mirabil consequenza'. There are nine ranks of angels, sub-divided into three triads of three. Each angelic order contemplates the Trinity in its own particular manner. Each likewise is related to one of the nine planetary heavens – so there is, after all, not merely physical life in the universe but the life of pure angelic intelligence, moving all creation, in diverse ways, to participate in creative Glory. The *mirabil consequenza* that astonishes but also animates the human eye is the unexpected congruence or exact correspondence between the largest of the planetary sphere – that which circles most widely – to the smallest in dimension, and therefore most intense, of the angelic orders.

So hierarchy is indeed a paradox – or better say a source of wonder. It is this response, in wonder, that leads us into the dancing life of the Trinity. That perichoresis is the life of the True Church; and Dante traces the energies and patterns of this life at marvellous length through the whole of the narrative and poetic implication of Canto 28. Below I offer just two instances of what the canto at large displays.

In the first of these passages, enumeration dissolves – and with all sense of higher and lower or more or less – into rhythms and patterns of a divine dynamism; and one notes the concluding neologism *s'invera* – to 'en-truth oneself – which points to those creative truths which respond not to calculation but to an exhilarating renewal of, precisely, participation:

> Around that point to similar extent
> fire in a circle whirled at such great speed
> its motion would surpass all clasped round earth.
>
> This was, in orbit, bounded by the next,
> by that a third, the third then by a fourth,
> by five that four and then by six that five.
>
> Then, round all these, a seventh ran, so stretched
> to generous breadth that Juno's messenger,
> the rainbow arc would hardly hold the all.
>
> Likewise, the eighth and ninth. And each of these
> moved still more slowly as the count went on,
> running, in number, outward from the one.
>
> And that possessed the clearest flame of all
> from which the purest spark stood least far off,
> because, I think, that flame in-truthed the most.

*Paradiso* 28: 23–39

In the second case, the poet takes the mystic number Three – always associated with the Trinity – and rhapsodizes or riffs on the possibility of relationship that the word opens up, as for example in another neologism 's'interna' to 'three' oneself internally – and the lovely, strange enjambment, after the *Hosanna* on the elongated word three itself – 'tree'. The final reference to 'angelici ludi' ('angelic games') associates the freedom of angelic activity with the lexical play of the poet himself:

> The second triad where the sap thus flows
> within this sempiternal springtime season –
> which night ascendant Aries never spoils –
>   sings out perpetually that winter's done
> 'Osanna!' in three tunes that sound in three
> orders of happiness, each en-threeing here.
>   The other gods in this hierarchic rank
> are firstly Dominations, Virtues next,
> then, thirdly, there's the Order of the Powers.
>   In three-some reels the two penultimates
> are Principalities, Archangels, too.
> The last of all is all Angelic games.

*Paradiso* 28: 115–126

The game that Canto 28 has set in motion continues, always evolving, over the five cantos that remain until the end of the *Commedia*. Polemic now dissolves into pure praise, and if there were time I would now turn to Cantos 31, 32 and 33, where in liturgy and doxology, Dante's Church is truly what a Church was always meant to be. These cantos – to be painfully brief – are centred on the figure of the Virgin Mary, as the luminous centre of an ecclesial community. Gathered around her is the whole congregation of the saints and the redeemed, now formed into the shape of a great white rose, all lines and hierarchical divisions now resolving into circles and folds. This is the nuptial flower that the Whore of Babylon so dreadfully pollutes. But now at last the saints are seen to possess the recognizably human lineaments – all illuminated by the *caritas* that they were originally created to display. And the dance now is the dance of eyes – of glances passing in recognition and prayer across and around the celestial formation. As Mary embodied Christ, so too does the ecclesial rose. And the angels are now compared to bees, flitting in grace between the human flower and the presence of its Creator.

> In form, then, as a rose, pure brilliant white,
> there stood before me now the sacred ranks
> that Christ, by His own blood, had made his bride.
> The other force [*the angels*] that flying sees and sings
> the glory that so stirs their love of Him –
> the goodness, too, that makes them all they are –
> came down , as might a swarm of bees that, first,
> en-flower themselves, returning, afterwards,
> to where their efforts are made sweet to taste.

*Paradiso* 31: 1–9

I wish I could engage you more fully in this wonderful crescendo. But in conclusion I want to turn back – against the obvious logic of the narrative – to the *Purgatorio*, the central canto in the *Commedia*-triad, and in particular to a sequence – in Canto 9 – where an angel, certainly, figures but where the main point of interest might be Dante's entry into the community of a penitent Church.

There are three main considerations underlying this final section.

The first of these involves an acknowledgement that, in the Reformation, the notion of Purgatory proved highly contentious. On the one hand, this notion invites us into a communion of prayer that includes the dead as well as the living. On the other hand, prayer for the dead can all-too easily degenerate into a trade in indulgences or into the ecclesial protection racket that Luther attacked so powerfully. Yet, as we have seen, Dante's devotion to the significance of Purgatory was great enough for him to override his detestation of Boniface and allow the efficacy of the papal pardon in the Jubilee of 1300 The question is whether – counter-factually – there would have been the need for any Reformation at all if Dante's highly original conception of Purgatory had been given proper attention.

A second consideration to raise here is that Purgatory, on Dante's view, involves not only the Mercy of God but also the work of human hands – *laborare* as well as *orare*. There are indeed those who would suggest that Dante verges on Pelagianism in stressing how, through the exercise of God-given potentialities, human souls are called upon in Purgatory to work out a salvation of their own: Dante's penitents positively and freely *choose* to be in Purgatory and likewise choose the moment at which they feel themselves to be free of sin.

The third reason behind this coda is almost entirely personal: the *Purgatorio*, it seems to me, is the most delicate part of the *Commedia* in both theological and poetic terms: it is here that his love of images in both the natural and the artistic sphere stimulates in him an awareness of how all the details of the created order may act as intermediaries between all human beings and their Creator. All things, in Dante's imagination, aspire to the condition of an icon.

In his conception of Purgatory Dante takes a doctrine which the Church had determined *as* a doctrine only a century or so (or more formally at the Council of Lyon in 1245) before he offered his own version and goes on to develop a model which has neither precedent not subsequent imitator.[3] Purgatory is for him no subterranean – though mercifully not eternal – form of Hell. That, roughly, was how Aquinas viewed it. Instead, Dante locates Purgatory as a mountainous island in the southern hemisphere, at the antipodes of Jerusalem, where natural time and natural meteorology all punctuate the penitential centuries that the souls – always assured of salvation – have to pass , rising progressively from one level to another.

In Canto 9 – after a day spent on the foothills of the mountain – Dante is ready to enter the Gate which leads into the realm of Purgatory-proper. And this is where we pick up the narrative.

Night has fallen and Dante, after the labours of the first day, has sunk into a fitful sleep. But then he begins to dream; and the dream seems terrifying: he imagines that a great golden eagle is circling above him. It swoops, seizes him and rises aloft through the fiery heavens as though this were the Eagle of

Jupiter and Dante were the helpless Ganymede. Now this, significantly, takes us back to our opening considerations of Imperial power. The Eagle must always stand symbolically for the Eagle of the Roman Empire, the embodiment of Divine Justice. So here, exercising a power which strikes initially as violence, the dream-bird may be seen to raise Dante aloft in the spirit of justice so that he is fit to enter salvation through the Gate of Purgatory – which one might also see as the Gateway to the True Church. Yet now in terror Dante awakes, and is told that there is no reason for terror at all. He has indeed been raised up and is now within sight of the Gate. But the power that he supposed was the power of an omnipotent Eagle was, he now learns, the gentle action of St Lucy, patron saint of light and Dante's own acknowledged patron – or matron – who had come to lift him child-like to the promised realm. Justice, it seems, is the way we first understand the action of Love; and the way ahead is ensured not by an Imperial march but rather by a maternal embrace.

Yet now the second phase of the action begins, which Dante must accomplish by his own efforts – by his own conscious and waking *work*. There are still three steps to climb; and terror is here renewed. For at the summit of this stair, guarding the entrance to Purgatory, there is an angel. This angel will indeed provide an intercessory link between the human and divine. But at first sight its presence no less alarming than, earlier, the Eagle had been. The vestments of the angels are the drab colour of ash. And two keys glint from beneath this robe as assurance – in a truly papal sense – of admission to the realm of salvation. Yet the angel also holds a sword which in the light of new day reflects a dazzling and dangerous gleam into Dante's eyes. What will this sword do once Dante arrives at the summit?

Indeed the climb itself towards this summit has terrors of its own. The first step shines with the clarity of a perfect mirror, so that Dante must see himself as truly he is – always a discomfiting experience. Then the second step erases that self-image. It is utterly black and its texture cracked in cruciform fissures.

Is the self to be recovered only through the kenosis of the cross? And the third step does restore us to humanity but, again, in a nerve-racking way. It is red porphyry – or, in Dante's phrase, the colour of 'blood spurting from a vein' – the marble itself speaks of a life which is, paradoxically, a life of pain and martyrdom.

Now, in an allegorical light, it is regularly supposed that these three steps are to be understood as the three formal phases in the sacrament of Confession. But too rapid a reading in allegorical terms would obscure the poetic theology that Dante's vibrant imagery itself here generates: our assimilation as participants in Divine Mercy is here attained through a willing abandonment of self, through an acceptance of the cross and then through an unshakeable re-connection – embodied as it were in marble – with our otherwise fragile humanity.

But Dante has still to meet the angel; and here as earlier – when the Eagle was revealed to be, in truth. St Lucy – nothing is exactly as our normal logic would suggest it should be. For the sword – so often the symbol of power – proves in its effect more to be a feather or even a quill pen than an instrument of domination. Dante presents his brow to the point of the sword. And the sword inscribes on Dante's flesh the letter *P* seven times over – *P* representing here both sin – *peccata* – and, equally *penitenza*, penitence. But there is no blood spurting now, nor any cry of anguish. The touch is gentle and redemptive; and Dante is told that once he has entered Purgatory the seven letters will progressively be washed from his forehead. As in a repeated act of baptism, the self now reconciled through Confession, is free to recover the self that it was always intended to be.

So now the Gate opens. It grinds and grates in a menacing fashion as if Dante were to be for ever locked within. And indeed he is. But he is now locked in to salvation. And mingling with sound of rusty hinges is the sound of the *Te Deum*, itself echoing the *Sanctus*, the hymn that was, in Luther's hands, to become a central feature of festive doxology:

We praise thee, O God: we acknowledge thee to be the Lord. All the earth doth worship thee: the Father everlasting. To thee all Angels cry aloud: the Heavens, and all the Powers therein. To thee Cherubim and Seraphim: continually do cry, Holy, Holy, Holy: Lord God of Hosts; Heaven and earth are full of thy Majesty.

# Notes

1   Foxe's work is quoted here from Paget Jackson Toynbee, *Dante in English literature from Chaucer to Cary (c. 1380-1844)*. (London [1909]). Other reformers are recorded by Toynbee as drawing on Dante (ibid p 56), for instance John Vander Noodt names Dante in a long list of 'reformers' (translated into English in 1569) that also includes Luther and Calvin.

2   John Milbank: 'Ecclesiology: The Last of the Last', in *Being Reconciled: Ontology and Pardon* (London, 2003).

3   The classic study of the history of Purgatory – which includes high praise for Dante's conception is Jacques Le Goof *La Naissance de Purgatoire* (Paris 1981).

# 4

# Luther and Church revisited

## *Robert Rosin*

In Lutheran Reformation circles, justification has been called the chief article on which all theology stands and falls – justification solely by God's grace come through faith alone in God's promises. This is the key point, the central truth of the evangelical Reformation spearheaded by Luther as he sought an answer to a very personal question: 'How do I find a God who loves me?' At the same time, this central point is not the only point revisited and reformed in the course of the sixteenth-century upheaval. The doctrine of the church also encountered heavy criticism and underwent major revision, not simply as an article of faith in its own right, but because of how that doctrine of the church stood in relationship to that central article of justification. It remains a key concept, because how we view 'church' can, as the sixteenth century discovered, affect the central feature of Lutheran, of biblical theology.

What is church? The *communion sanctorum*? An/the institution? The gathered priesthood of believers? What does Luther have to say about church, its nature, and its structure? More precisely, what does Luther want for a *sine qua non*, that is, what is the absolute or the bottom line when it comes to how the church should exist, look, and be ordered or organized both in Luther's day and ours? There actually is a simple answer to at least some of that. But before that there is some groundwork to be laid and some rough spots to manage while talking about church. Along with marshaling historical facts and texts with which to work, we are saddled with the passage of time and a change of circumstances.[1] What do we do when so much of what was said in Luther's day reflects a given historical or cultural circumstance? That does not close the door to understanding, but it does remind us that context counts.

It would be presumptuous to speak for Lutheranism in Britain, but in the USA – more familiar turf – some in our circles are quick to absolutize Luther's thoughts from beginning to end, as if to freeze the sixteenth century and carry it over to present day. At times they act as if there are no differences. At others they will privilege Luther's era and bemoan their own and then act as if by quoting Luther a few times and wishing this were the sixteenth century we could make it so. That's the myth of the golden age. And while there arguably are advantages to some parts of the sixteenth century (and in fact, some of my best friends live in the sixteenth century!), we cannot build booths on that mountaintop any more than Peter, James, and John could freeze time and make the Transfiguration a relic. In truth, this golden age likely never existed and resembles a foreign country in more ways than one, a time and place imagined in sepia tones, even as the nostalgia is weaponized, at the ready to be unleashed.

But while some work to reverse time, others are just as quick to argue that because times have changed, virtually nothing from Luther's day is transferable. History then becomes no more than a depository of the past with no carryover to the present. At best, history can set the table, but it has nothing of substance to contribute other than examples of what we ought not to do today. As often happens, however, it seems the truth is in the middle and is more complex than either of those other alternatives.

We cannot ignore past circumstances or isolate ourselves from culture – Luther's or our own – any more than we can cease breathing and avoid the air around. Culture is understood broadly as anything nonbiological that we create consciously or not. It is simply part of the world in which we live. Yet it is important to keep priorities in mind when looking at theology and cultural worldviews. Who is shaping the message? Do we live in the world and engage it, or do we succumb to its pressures and become of the world, allowing it to dictate the theological message? There is no avoiding context. Again, context counts. Context often poses questions when it comes to theology; it offers challenges and highlights problems. If we do not listen to the context, we risk answering questions not asked and ignoring others. But when Christians listen and respond, they must work within context without letting context be the tail that wags the dog.

Better to strive for a balance, striving to hear both message and context and then attempt to bridge the gap.[2] As a colleague put it, the point is to preserve the integrity of the message while integrating it into the context at hand. That's not always easy, but it is essential to be fair both to the message and the audience.[3]

As noted at the start, for the Lutheran Reformation justification by grace alone through faith alone was the cornerstone on which all that follows stands or falls. But church and its place in theology are not far away from this center. The *sola gratia* and *sola fide* message was rooted ultimately in a reading, in the foundation, of Scripture alone – *sola scriptura*. By taking Scripture as his ultimate authority, his *norma normans* or norming norm, Luther seemed to signal the destruction of the place and purpose of the church as it then was. Whatever survived certainly would not resemble the pre-Reformation era in terms of the concept of the church or in terms of the church's place and purpose. From the point where Luther was thrust on the international scene in the late 1510s and early 1520s, his position on soteriology, on sacraments, on virtually any topic also necessarily touched on the matter of the church, on its nature and so also on its authority and structure, two issues intimately bound together.

As things began, Luther tried to speak in conservative, respectful ways, honoring both ecclesiastical authority and structure. His 95 Theses, for example, were issued in a standard fashion,[4] with Luther proposing a debate within the university community where his ideas could be challenged, refined, or refuted. But concerned about the indulgence sales, Luther saw this as more than a hypothetical university exercise. He hoped to reach beyond the university setting, so Luther also delivered his theses to his ecclesiastical superiors, taking a best construction approach, presuming they did not know how indulgences were hawked and hoping the abuses would be corrected. Even when the furor erupted, Luther worked within the structures. To be sure, he defended himself against the polemicists and gave as good as he got. It seems crude, but that was just the way public disputes were handled. There is nothing out of the ordinary here. More important, in Luther's exchanges with various church officials he followed recognized procedures. He may have become exasperated, disappointed, or disillusioned, but Luther gave structure a chance.

At the same time, structure was sure to come in for criticism because the church was advocating a position that Luther found fundamentally incompatible with the grace and faith message the word seemed to proclaim, and that was a problem, a threat for what in Luther's mind really was the essence of the church. This clash of church and Reformation theology could not be fixed with a bit of tinkering because the church's conception of both itself and its structure was essentially part of the problem. In other words, Luther came to see it was impossible to keep the concept and structure of the church as he had come to know it while simply substituting a different message. That would be a case of new wine in old wine skins. Rome had made itself a part of the old message and if the message was reformed, the church in terms of concept and structure also would have to be reformed, because it did not serve church as the communion of saints, the believers in Christ.

Luther may have begun by giving the church all due respect, but very quickly in the public battle, ecclesiastical authority and structure were smashed beyond repair. In the past, some such as the conciliarists had sought to salvage elements of the church and bring about some new constitutional form. There was no wholesale housecleaning but rather more a rebuilding with the same parts while substituting a new emphasis for the old. Even the most radical of late medieval conciliarists never conceived of the church without the episcopal hierarchy or papacy, for example.[5] Instead they wanted a new balance. The church as the collected wisdom gathered in council through whom the Spirit worked would still give rise to the message. For Luther, however, the converse was true: the message, that is, the word, created the church in whatever manifestation, form, or structure it would have.

How well did Luther's opponents understand his point? That's difficult to say. Certainly they quickly grasped that their present structure was under attack. Both committed, old-style papists and holdovers from conciliarism could easily see that. But could they grasp how radically Luther was reversing the relationship of church and word? The old thinking expected that even if the church were severely flawed, it would still somehow reconstitute itself and then be the arena for the shaping of God's message. It (re)presented a continuing revelation, the voice of God. Were any of Luther's critics prepared to go all the way with Luther and see that structure was generate*d* rather than generat*ing*, that structure was created rather than creative or creating? That is difficult to answer, though it is easy to imagine that most could never conceive of the church as Luther did. Something had to stand as the guarantor of the message, and that was church (or papacy – nearly the same thing).

But for Luther, the church and its structure are not the subject but rather stand in the predicate as the word is proclaimed and gives rise to church. 'Paradigm shift' is a much overused term, and many do not understand all that the expression entails, but if ever the term could be applied, here is a classic case – a paradigm shift of mammoth proportions in thinking, a great reversal that Luther precipitated.[6] Luther himself may not have grasped everything as it unfolded, especially where things might end in terms of the structure that might emerge as the message was proclaimed, but he certainly understood enough (and more than those around him) to know that if the Gospel should be preached in this way, the church as most saw the institution would never be the same.

We could hunt for headwaters earlier in Luther,[7] but it is enough for now to note that church and its structure very quickly emerged near the center of the discussion. As noted, in issuing his 95 Theses Luther still showed respect for the structure. So do Luther's contacts with those authorized to handle his case. Frustration and his *Bedenken* aside, Luther worked though channels. He dutifully went to Heidelberg in 1518 to offer his thoughts for review and debate, a churchly thing to do for his fellow Augustinians, who were bound to be targets with guilt by association.[8] As Luther laid out issues of sin and grace, the lack of free will, and advocated a theology of the cross rather than a theology of glory when it came to the matter of saving faith and the Christian life, church structure served as an outlet, but it did not determine the substance.

If Luther had thought the church then might have been an agent for reform, he soon abandoned that notion as the controversy grew, and by 1519 he publicly targeted the church, specifically its structure. In the past some would-be reformers had complained about abuses in the church and had looked to the head, the papacy, to lead reform. Others, the conciliarists, had complained about problems with the head, though the larger body still offered hope. Some even would call the pope the 'antichrist' – the papal see had certainly heard the term before! But while conciliarists could squabble among themselves about particulars, they still saw themselves as the overseers (bishops) and theologians who would assemble to be the salvation of the church in the end. But what should people on either side – papist or conciliarist – make of Luther once they heard him at the Leipzig Debate in 1519? In letters Luther had suggested he did not know if the pope was the antichrist or only his agent, but that sort of stuff could be dismissed as an aftershock from conciliarism. But at Leipzig with John Eck's prodding, Luther went farther: not only popes but also councils can and have erred.[9] Really? How about an example? Luther obliged not by arguing some technical administrative issue or some gray area of judgment. No, Luther cited the condemnation of John Hus and his message as just such an error.[10]

With that dramatic example, Luther left himself little room to work with church and structure as most had come to know it. This was no accidental, isolated outburst, however, and no unfortunate misstep. Luther deepened his criticisms the next year. In his 'Appeal to the Christian Nobility' he launched a frontal assault on the church and its structure.[11]

Rome huddled behind three walls in defense of its status before God and its privilege in this world, but Luther battered through all three. Rome's first line of defense distinguished sacred and secular vocations, with those within the church holding a special place in sacred, God-pleasing callings, keeping church things in church hands, defending the institution said to be superior and so authoritative. All others draw nigh and hear.

But Luther took a radical approach. True, bishops ought to provide leadership. (Whether there have to be bishops in the end is another issue to be discussed later.) But the simple presence of bishops is no guarantee of truth or that things will go right. In fact, when bishops fail to provide oversight, when they abrogate their responsibility. What then? Then princes and those in ruling authority must step up and lead – a different structure come to the rescue. Princes are not clerics, but seen in light of the fourth commandment and thinking of the people as family and the princes and civil leaders as father figures, those in ruling authority ought to seek out the best for their families, including the best spiritual leadership possible. For Luther, the best meant promoting evangelical reform.[12] If clergy charged with spiritual care will provide that, then princes can support and encourage them in their efforts. If clergy refuse or fail, then princes must fill the gap. True, they likely have no theological expertise, but they can find, install, and support those who do. Here are Luther's *Notbischöfe*, his 'emergency bishops' – clearly not something Rome included in its flow charts.[13]

What a radical notion! The institution defended itself by throwing up a wall, vertically separating sacred vocations on one side and secular on the other. Luther reoriented things: now there is no difference between the vocations themselves – God-pleasing versus all others. Now the difference is between the people themselves who fill the vocations, people whose hearts God sees. Faith's presence, not the vocation per se, is the issue. And the bishop who obstructs the truth does no good work. Regardless of how pious people think his vocation or office might be, he has not acted in faith. Whether intended for good by well-meaning supporters or maintained in self-defense by those guarding their privilege, that wall shoring up the structure simply will not stand Luther's onslaught.[14]

In razing the sacred/secular wall, Luther assured that church structure would remain a hot issue. At Leipzig Luther's critics saw him climb far out on a limb. With this treatise, he has sawed the limb off – so thought his opponents. Luther, however, saw things differently: the tree is structurally and organically rotten and cannot hope to stand. So the ax was even now being laid to the root. Critics might not care if Luther himself came crashing down, but as he battered away at the walls of the church, he threatened serious damage. In his critics' eyes, Luther has given the sacred authority of the church over to profane hands. But Luther was not through. He would not only breach the wall, he would set fire to the structure's foundations.

When old buildings are renovated, walls might be temporarily torn down, but something will have to stabilize the structure, and the walls will have to be built back. Walls would seem to be essential to the integrity of the structure. Looking at itself in Luther's day, church was not satisfied with just any sort of wall. Authority in clerical hands was loadbearing. It defined church even as other ideas leaned on it. More, the structure of church was defended as being primary to and independent of key articles of faith and so held priority. If that were not bad enough, church structure was turned to deal with Luther and his message, aiming to silence.

So Luther struck back and burned the foundations of the walls he had smashed, torching them, so to speak, when he burned the papal bull outside Wittenberg's Elster Gate in December 1520. The students stoked the flames with copies of the canon law, the rulebooks of the structure. There was no thought salvaging the old – minor editing was out of the question and even major revisions would not do when it came to these rules. No matter how they might cut, paste, and rework the canon law, the attitude behind it posed a deeper problem as the institution pictured itself as the generator of thought and conduct, a priori to faith and life. More than the rules, it was all that lay behind the rules in terms of structure that made the blaze burn bright. Put simply, the view of structure being prior and independent ruled out any further use of these rules, because with that attitude, the rules had overshadowed the Gospel.

Luther did not shy from the bonfire or stand in the way of the students. In fact, he helped feed the flames with the papal bull, whose authority presumed the structure he had already attacked. Copies of the canon law – more on order and process – already had gone up in smoke. The gesture made crystal-clear his rejection of church structure for identity and definition, and it confirmed in the minds of some former supporters that Luther had gone too far. Before he captured the wider public eye, Luther had been known to many of the intellectuals and was familiar to the German humanists who had followed his efforts at Wittenberg where in the years before the Reformation upheaval, he had been a prime mover urging a shift to the 'New Learning' of Renaissance humanism in the university curriculum. Humanism's emphasis on the classical liberal arts rose to rival and then supplant scholasticism's stranglehold through Aristotle's syllogistic logic and dialectic. Humanists elsewhere watched with interest, and Luther's reputation grew.[15]

But the older humanists did not realize the depth of Luther's insight or the theological implications of what he was about. And then there was the impact this would have on the church, including with matters of structure. (To be fair, at this early date, Luther probably did not know either where this all would end up, but he knew he was not tinkering around the edges.) Luther's reform of method at the university – the shift from scholasticism's logic and dialectic to humanism's exposition of texts using language and grammar – was the most important focus that would have an impact more than morality and personal piety. The reform of exegetical method and presuppositions would bring radical change in theology, and theology would change structure. Here is a truism beyond the Reformation: presuppositions and method always affect the outcome; change the approach and you change the product, theology included.

If others missed the point, Luther certainly knew the significance of these changes. In a 1518 letter to his old teacher Trutfetter, Luther laid his cards on the table as reform swept through: 'I believe simply that it is impossible to reform the church if the canons, the decretals, the scholastic theology, the philosophy, the logic as they now stand are not uprooted and another study installed.'[16] Theological presuppositions and method and also the larger structure (the canons and decretals) are completely out – 'uprooted', Luther says. The structure of the church was standing in the way of honest, true theology. It set itself up first and sought then to determine the message, the truth. Even without the Elster Gate bonfire and its light, Luther had seen the canons and decretals in a new light, standing in obstruction rather than in service to the truth. Here is an important principle recognized early by Luther: theology, the proclamation and hearing of the word, is paramount, and structure must serve that end. Put a bit differently, theology creates and defines church. The institution or structure is not the driver. At the same time, note a couple of things Luther has not said. He has not argued that having structure is in and of itself a problem, or that having structure will automatically damage the use of the word. Luther is no categorical ecclesiastical anarchist. Nor, on the other hand, has Luther suggested here that there is some mandated church structure or an ideal form, although we do know that Rome, as it existed, could not be salvaged and instead needed a major overhaul. What should we make of this? Is Luther's lack of discussion shortsighted, or could this be wishful thinking on Luther's part, expecting or hoping that structural problems would take care of themselves?

To this point we have explored two major attacks Luther launched against church structure. First, he argued that popes and councils can and have erred. That is, the simple existence of church offices and ecclesiastical structure is no guarantee that all is done correctly and produces right results. We know this because of the second blow Luther struck by rejecting the canons and decretals themselves. So Luther repudiates both the long history of the institution and the very rules on which the church rests and by which it functions.

But Luther is not through. He unleashed a third blow at what remained of church structure. With an emphasis on 'by grace alone' and 'by faith alone', the mediating role for church structure gave way to the priesthood of all believers. If each of God's baptized is a priest standing immediately before God for Christ's sake, then there is no absolute need for some church structure or no essential requirement for some organization that must exist above the individual. There is no fundamental need for those high on the ecclesiastical ladder, and no need either for a priest to be an intermediary or an intercessor, that is, for a priest to offer sacrifice (the sacrifice of the mass) on behalf of the people. Instead each believer as a priest can offer thanksgiving in words and life for the saving grace already given. This means, in short, that structure cannot stand between the believer and God, though that was just what was happening in Luther's day. Luther's favorite motif for justification, the 'happy exchange' (*commercium admirabile*), accents the relationship. In the exchange, Christ takes the sinner's place and assumes all that goes with that label 'sinner': guilt, rejection by the Father, death, and hell – and that all becomes properly Christ's ('made sin for us,' Paul writes). And on the other hand, the sinner leaves all that behind and takes Christ's place. In baptism, Christ's name is put on the individual, and with that name comes all the name stands for: the Father's love rather than rejection, life rather than death, and the closest, most immediate relationship one can have with the Father. If this is so, then what need is there of a structure to stand in between? And what should we think of a structure that insists on forcing itself into the picture and claim a place in this relationship? The structure Luther saw epitomized in Rome existed to control. It was not needed but claimed a right to broker salvation. That made structure a matter of Law rather than Gospel, but we know the higher relationship with God exists always and only in the Gospel. No wonder Luther struck out at Rome. This relationship between the sinner/believer and God is the most important one that exists, not a relationship between the believer and some structure or between some structure and God. If Luther is serious about the 'happy exchange', then the church structure that Luther saw simply was neither necessary nor essential but actually could do damage.

Here is Luther's three-prong attack from early in the reform movement. Popes and councils, that is, those in the structure, can err. Having structure is no guarantee that all is well. Beyond that, the canons and decretals have to go, because they have propped up a church structure that has blocked the Gospel. Remember Luther's 1518 letter: presuppositions, method, and the canons and decretals of the structure must be replaced with a very different approach to theology. And to finish the attack, the priesthood of all believers means there is no need for ecclesiastical structure to stand before God. If those supporting structure say otherwise, they are imposing Law where the Gospel had cleared the field. All this adds up to Luther's rejection of the ecclesiastical structure as he had come to know it. It was not simply a matter of the structure being plagued by problems in that historical context. The way the structure argued its right to existence, its place among believers and before God, made structure in that sense unacceptable in any context. It rivaled the Gospel.

But despite all this criticism, Luther never lost sight of the church – what it is, where it can be found, and how it might be ordered. But church now is recast. It stands as a living organism, for it is made of living people of faith.

At this point it may seem that Luther has destroyed the church. That is only a problem if one thinks institutionally in terms of formal or de facto structures. But Luther continued to confess the creeds with the 'holy catholic/Christian church'. The truth is that for Luther, 'church' is not that complicated a concept or that difficult to find. Faced with the possibility of a church council in Mantua in 1537 (which did not come to be – wait instead until Trent), Luther described church in the Smalcald Articles, a document that might have been offered at Mantua. He put is simply: a seven-year-old child knows what church is, namely, the sheep who hear the voice of the shepherd Christ.

So much is recast in Luther's thinking on the church. The old structure taught about saints above who were said to intervene with help for us below. That was supposed to give comfort. But Luther saw a different role for saints and found comfort elsewhere. Saints are first the believers in this life who are holy by God's grace from their baptism on through their lives of faith. True comfort comes in seeing God's promises that create faith and preserve life. Saints comfort but only in a secondary way: not by intervening but by serving as examples of how God also works with believers now, promising and preserving. Their lives encourage. Those saints above already taken to be with God and those saints still living by saving grace here below combine to make the church for Luther.[17] They are the 'communion of saints' of the creed. This is the church, with a life and essence not dependent on structure but with believers tied to Christ and encouraged by one another in a bond of faith, linked by the Gospel that makes all things new. We sometimes refer to this as the *unio mystica*, the mystical union. But this is not intended to reduce the church to some ethereal, imaginary bond as if we could never see this communion in action. Of course the real key will be the marks of the church (more to come on that) and no human being knows who truly is holy, that is, who truly believes. God alone sees the heart. Yet while hypocrites can fool us, it is hard to imagine that everything we hear and see is a sham, though some surely is. So the church is said to be hidden or concealed.[18]

Luther was pushed to this thinking when faced with Rome's insistence on the historic, visible structure, but we should not think this was simply Luther being contrary. Eck was able to tar him with the Hussite label when Luther called the church 'the body of the elect', but Luther was not so clumsy as to be forced into a definition he had not considered and was stuck defending.[19] And while Luther stressed the inwardness and spirituality of the church, especially in contrast to the physical assembly of Rome, he did not leave 'church' simply as an abstract, esoteric idea. Rather it existed in reality and was all around.

Far from being bound to any particular place, persons, or time, church cut across all of these as a larger spiritual union, believers with the word rooted in their hearts – no abstract idea but a reality. But while believers are evidence of the church, it is not their creation or theirs (or clerics or bishops) to rule.

The church is certainly not bound to any particular place, person, or time. In fact, it cuts across all of these – again a larger spiritual union. Believers in any time or place are in the church because the word has taken root in their hearts and makes the church a reality, but note: believers are not what make the church what it is. As Luther wrote, 'Christ's kingdom is governed by the solid and simple word of the Gospel.'[20] Luther again: 'The church's whole life and substance is in the word of God.'[21] The Gospel is the substance of the church, not the believers. Believers are made what they are by the Gospel and therefore are the church. The church will exist as long as Christ exists. That is a very different approach than Luther had seen in the church with its substance resting on its structure and historical existence.

The proclaimed Christ, the Gospel (and not believers) stand as the maker and substance of the church, evidence of the Holy Spirit's work described in the Small Catechism's Third Article. Abstract? Hardly. Christ and the Gospel create the church, which is very real and can be found alive in the world, not off in some distant realm of ideas. Where? Where the signs or marks are to be found. Said Luther, 'For some visible sign has to be given by which means we are to be gathered into one body in order to hear the word of God.'[22] Those signs are the sacraments and especially the Gospel, three things about which Christians ought to agree.[23] (That is just what Melanchthon echoes in Article VII of the Augsburg Confession.) While church spans history and geography, if one wants to know where it is, look (and listen): the signs or marks are right before one's eyes. (Is this a bit of Luther's nominalism with an emphasis on immediacy: at hand rather than distant in thought?)

Within this trio of Baptism, Lord's Supper, and proclamation of the Gospel, Luther is especially focused on the last. This is not to denigrate the other two but rather recognizes the relationship. First, the two sacraments with the promise of saving, forgiving grace, do indeed create faith and make the church. But this tends to happen in a corporate setting. Gatherings are likely smaller with Baptism when families, not wanting to wait given infant mortality in that day, bring newborns during the week. And the Lord's Supper, while frequent, occurs during a corporate service. But speaking the Gospel – admonishing with Law and especially comforting and forgiving with Gospel, ideally happens at any time of the day, any day of the week, within family and community whenever there is opportunity for a natural and proper exercise of the priesthood of the baptized. (Remember: no sacred/secular wall.) Second, while the proclamation of the Gospel is easy on one hand, on the other it can be easily distorted. Hence Luther's point that false proclamation can also rob the other signs or marks (Sacraments) of their meaning, reducing them to empty ceremonies or rituals while the salvific promise is lost.

Even if that is avoided, it is not enough to have the word correctly written down on paper, there for the record. Rather it must be proclaimed – the spoken word of the Gospel (*verbum evangelii vocale*).[24] As Luther once described the church, it is not a 'pen house' but rather a 'mouth house'. In other words, theology does not reside collected in books on the shelf. It has to be proclaimed, spoken, and used to address people in terms of Law and Gospel.[25] True theology is never finally theory but also practice, and the chief practice is proclamation.

When that proclamation occurs, the church is formed as the word works in people. Luther's opponent Thomas Murner charged Luther with teaching that the church was a platonic state or a utopia.[26] Instead Luther inseparably linked the real or spiritual dimension and the physical church. God's working faith in hearts that God alone sees might be invisible, but evidence of that divine working is certainly seen in people's lives. That working of faith is a glorious thing hidden from people as God's face was from Moses. And when others, particularly those in the world critical of God, look at the church it may look anything but glorious: 'The face of the church is the face of one who is a sinner – vexed, forsaken, dying, and distressed.'[27] Not a pretty picture, but that still is the church, and faith knows it. But where is the enabling structure in all that? – nowhere to be seen. Whether the church is called invisible, spiritual, abscondite or hidden, faith knows where the church is to be found by looking for the signs or marks. And when the word is proclaimed, faith knows what it has heard and knows it is home.

The image and power of 'church' in Luther's day was immense if one looked toward Rome. But for Luther the glory of the church lay not in structure, rules, or organization with a well-drawn flow chart. The glory is found rather in the communion of saints (*communio sanctorum*). Some sort of sociological reality can follow as Christians live together, but that is a product of God's working in them. The glory of the church is not bound to any particular person, place, time, or external thing of our making. It cannot exist without people like Peter (not to mention the other apostles who proclaimed the word), but Peter does not form the foundation of the church for Luther. Rather the church rests on what was said by Peter at Caesarea Philippi: 'You are the Christ ...' Where precisely that church will be found is impossible to forecast, but since witness to/of Christ is an ongoing activity, so long as Christ exists, the church exists.

This is not to argue for some uninterrupted or unbroken line, although it is difficult to imagine the world without some evidence of the church being present. But Luther would allow that it is at least possible for darkness to come until the Spirit works faith again.[28] (Think Ezekiel and dry bones.) While an unbroken line might be nice, it risks making the line the focus rather than an active, working word.

In the Apology of the Augsburg Confession, Melanchthon wrote in Article IV that the church is no 'association of external things and rites as are other states but it principally is an association of faith and the Holy Spirit in the hearts, which nevertheless has external marks.'[29] But even though Melanchthon expressly distinguishes the church from other sociological or political creations, the marks need to be used, and so the temptation exists to think our organizing and maneuvering of these (structure!) ought to share the spotlight.

That said, this does not mean Luther cared nothing about what is going on, as if we can just preach or proclaim any old thing under a label of word and sacrament and let God sort things out in people's hearts. In 1533 Luther wrote to Christians in Frankfurt am Main that whoever knew his pastor taught as Zwingli did should avoid him and sooner do without the sacrament throughout his life than receive it from this Zwinglian, even to the point of dying for this confession. As Luther said, 'it frightens me to hear that in one church or at one altar both groups [Lutheran and Zwinglian] should seek and receive one sacrament, and one group should believe that it receives only bread and wine, but the other should believe it receives the true body and blood of Christ. I often doubt it is credible that a preacher or pastor could be so stubborn and wicked that he remain silent about this and let both groups continue in this way, each in its own opinion.'[30] The point of caring about this confession is not because people create anything with their own rules and organization, but that God creates the church through the word, and people want to have a right confession of that word. It would be much easier to work with the rules of ecclesiastical polity instead of emphasizing doctrinal unity. But that was how Luther saw things.

Rome had claimed catholicity for itself because of Peter at Caesarea Philippi, its long history, and its privileged position protected by the Empire. But Luther's reform broke that bond as people became convinced that the church depends on the Gospel for its existence and its identity apart from institutional history or cultural position. With competing voices criticizing the status quo it became increasingly difficult for Rome to argue it was custodian of the catholic confession. Catholicity came from God through the word, Luther argues. He would even go so far as to call the papacy a sect, and other Reformers distinguished between 'Christians' (meaning the supporters of the Augsburg Confession) and 'papists'.[31] Nothing had changed in terms of structure, but Rome was having a more difficult time. It ought to give no one pleasure, and 'sectarian' is not a label to be used lightly. While organizations are not the solution and can bring problems that impinge on the message, they should not be dismissed too quickly. They may help. But they hinder when they trump message with structure.[32] The appeal to structure continued at and after the close of Luther's life with Trent, where structure was revisited and lines drawn more tightly.[33]

The Radical Reformation is, for Luther, kin to Rome in some ways, although the Radicals themselves argued that it was Rome and Lutherans who stood together on one side, while they fashioned themselves as the faithful remnant. (No surprise there.) For Luther, the Radicals problem was not simply or finally their structure but especially their message. Their misunderstanding of the Gospel prompted Luther's criticism, not the fact that they organized on a small scale on the local level. At the same time, that organizing was not divorced from their message. Many thought that by defining their lives together, by guarding their morality and purging those declared unworthy, they could do their part in building the kingdom of God. Here again is an emphasis on structure rather than on the signs of Gospel and sacraments. Radicals may view Rome with contempt, but in creating a community where, they believed, God might arrive at any time, rather like descending Jacob's ladder to usher in the new age, they had to bend the word to support their community and goals. In broad terms, for Luther that bending was what Rome did as well. One opponent looked small, local, and simple, while the other was huge, international, and extravagant, but both relied on structure. In the end, Rome and the Radicals are cut from the same cloth, both working to create their identities rather than be shaped by the word. But at the same time, while Luther could be critical, he could resort to pulling rank as well, at times treating the Reformation as his Reformation. It might not be what he would like to do, but in the upheaval of this revolution, it sometimes simply is easier to insist on something because of who he was. Luther did his best to keep his eye on the high road and see the work of a de facto bishop as service to the word doing its job, but the challenges and his efforts serve to remind how difficult it was (and is) to live as church within the parameters and with the model Luther championed. Gospel and forgiveness would apply to Luther's side as well.[34]

All this sounds so negative. Are there no upbeat take-aways from a look at Luther and church? Perhaps the best is simply what Luther did not do. Rather than substitute one structure for another, Luther argued for the word being preached to the joy and edifying of God's people. That proclamation happens among all believers who have the happy task or privilege of speaking the word to one another. But concern for proclamation also leads to the office of the public ministry. The connection of the ordained priesthood and the universal priesthood of believers (or the baptized) is a rich topic, but one that must wait for another time, another symposium. There are, however, some basic ideas that tie in with the church and structure issues at hand.

The Augsburg Confession (Article V) roots the ministry, the preaching office, in the doctrine of justification: 'In order that we may attain this faith, the ministry of teaching the Gospel and administering the sacraments has been instituted.' There are not two foundations but one for two ways in which the word is spoken. So the public ministry does not exist independently or function on its own, and it has no purpose except to serve the Gospel and the people who need to hear it. There can be no preacher or pastor without a message to preach but also none without people to whom he ministers. Those in the public office serve the people as a whole, the congregation – Sunday morning, to shorthand things. But that does not mean other Christians retire to the sidelines of life. They speak to one another. More, Luther argues that a Christian in the midst of nonbelievers must 'preach to the erring heathen or non-Christians and must teach the Gospel since brotherly love makes doing this his duty.' Even apart from this mission situation, Christians are 'duty bound to proclaim, teach, and spread' the word. Circumstances may vary but the task is the same.[35]

But the duty and desire to proclaim must also be balanced by the right to do so, particularly with the public office. So Christians, mindful of the expectations of the preaching office as Paul described them, choose someone to fill the office.[36] This is not something an individual can arrogate or take on oneself, then imposing that order on the believers.[37] That would make this an office of the Law, not Gospel. So the preaching office is a function that serves the congregation. The ministry is not something people pragmatically created. Rather, Luther argues, Christ established the ministry and gave it to the church, which then fills it. The ministry does not make the church any more than the believers created the ministry on their own, but that ministry also cannot exist without people. Here Luther is rather fluid with his terms – for example, with election, call, and ordination – and is also flexible on how those activities are carried out. An individual can be elected, that is chosen out of a group of qualified individuals by the theological faculty, and then a call is given. Or the person could be specifically requested (often the home congregation). That is just a start of a myriad of options and paths to service. What matters finally is that the person assumes the call, and about the only thing Luther is insistent on is that ordination does not impart any special or sacramental character. Instead it is a public signifying that the person has indeed been called and put in the public office.

But does this not require rules and procedures – structure? Yes and no. Here again Luther is fluid. First, the congregation, that is, the church in that place, is the focal point with a public ministry to fill. They may elect or they may rely on others with insight to do the electing and yet they may still examine the individual on their own. Luther urges bishops or superintendents to work with the people to find a good fit rather than impose someone whom the bishop wants there. Luther sided with the people of Leisnig when church officials dragged their feet. The title of Luther's 1523 treatise makes plain what he thinks: *That a Christian Assembly or Congregation Has the Right and Power to Judge All Teaching and to Call, Appoint, and Dismiss Teachers, Established and Proven by Scripture.*[38]

At the same time, a congregation is not the only expression of church and does not exist independently of other congregations that equally are expressions of church in other places. Luther's rather matter-of-fact way of providing for visitation of congregations show that he does not see a congregation having a right to exist in isolation on its own. Augsburg Confession XIV speaks of a cleric being 'rightly called' (*rite vocatus*), that is, called in good order as those involved have agreed and know it should be done. There is no one-size-fits-all procedure, but rather an adapting to local custom and practice. Doing things decently and in order is the bottom line. So it is clear that there is a need for procedures, but these do not define church but rather stand in service of the church as a way of providing for the word and sacraments.[39] And there were ways to move clerics should that seem best for all concerned – no job for life. How someone came to a particular office was not as important as the attitude and abilities that came with the person. Heading into the Reformation, bishops did not have to be clerics but they had to be administrators, and so when a noble's first son inherited the title and lands, the second and third sons could still rule, but they would do it within the institutional church. Ruling might be appropriate given the responsibility on that level, but the pastor ought to keep Christ, his cross, and his love before the people's eyes. If that did not happen, someone else could be found to serve.[40]

Out of baptized Christians people are called into public ministry as pastors, and at the same time the baptized are relating to congregations around them to live in the larger body of Christ. That would seem to call for order and regularity, so what should they have for church structure? Luther really does not care, so long as they understand that the Gospel makes the church what it is, that the people stand before God as priests, and Christ would have them have a pastor not to mediate, not to rule, but rather to feed them the word. Beyond that, how they work out their relationships with one another and how they provide in good order for the ministry to be filled is of no interest to Luther. What matters is that the Gospel is served and Christ's people are served by whatever is done. Whatever structure results is fine, so long as no one presumes that defines the church and establishes its identity everywhere. Structure is never an a priori prescription but rather exists a posteriori, growing out of the Gospel's activity. Structure ought to acknowledge freely that it follows out of the identity that the Gospel creates. Within that structure, people must continue to deal with one another on the basis of the Gospel – not easy to do when problems arise. Would it not be simpler to quote a rule and exercise power? But Luther will not have it. Even when hard decisions must be made and rough edges remain, these must point beyond the moment, giving witness to and serving the Gospel.

We might like Luther to be more prescriptive when it comes to church, to draw up a clear set of rules, or to select one tight structure to follow, but he will not. He is far too busy trying to get people to see the Gospel in all its richness. The world bemoans what seem like sloppy procedures, loose ends, and ambiguities within the visible church and with Luther's comments, but Luther is willing to live with that. After all, it is a privilege to work with the baptized children, with the royal priests of Christ. Besides, time is flying by, and the bridegroom might return at any moment. As a historian friend once quipped, apocalyptic thinking does not lend itself to long-range planning.

So what to do? Will 'pack light and move quickly' work today with all that needs to be done? Well, given the slide seen in business-as-usual institutional Christianity with legacy church bodies, it is worth a try. Some will never give up on booth building, as they search for a particular model that is sure to be the silver bullet, or so they hope. They often seek to reach back to some golden age as if they could pull forward a past that surely (?) will succeed. But while a model may have worked once, there is no guarantee it will again. If the plan stalls, then circle the wagons, look inward, and congratulate one another for being part of a faithful remnant.

Granted, life is not easy as Luther sees things with the devil, the world, and one's own fallen nature confounding matters and upending the best-laid plans. So rather than trying to sort through and put right the world (a Sisyphean task), far better to keep it simple while on the way to the new heaven and the new earth. On the way, church is the place to be. That is simple, too, for Luther. Remember his line from the Smalcald Articles: a seven-year-old child knows what the church is, namely, the sheep who hear the voice of the shepherd. Presumably those who hear will follow. To where? It really does not matter if the shepherd leads. Long and winding journeys can cause grumbling, so beware. Israel had its episodes during its forty years, but do not sour on the journey. Better to look ahead, to watch for all things new, to treat those around as fellow pilgrims, and to welcome more to come along. A simple suggestion comes from Giorgio Agamben in *The Church and the Kingdom*.[41] God called on Old Israel to welcome strangers to join the ranks and travel with them – something they could do with grace because of grace showed to them. Nothing really is different for the New Israel, the church. With so much in flux, structures matter little. Gospel proclamation is all that matters. The travelers need only be true to their identity: royal priests with a task to remind, to proclaim to one another and more around. Luther understands this is not complicated. So enjoy and get on with it.

# Notes

1   David Lowenthal has written two books that show the enormity of the gap between 'back then' and the present day. His first: *The Past Is a Foreign Country* (Cambridge: Cambridge University Press, 1986), and the second: *The Past Is a Foreign Country— Revisited* (Cambridge: Cambridge University Press, 2015). Lowenthal explains in the preface to the second volume that he had intended to start from the platform of his 1986 book and then add and tweak material, notes, and bibliography. But so much had changed in nearly thirty years that he decided instead to write a second book. If three decades can prompt that, 500 years since the Reformation ought to foster caution.

2   On the intersection of Christianity and culture, the message and its context, see Robert Rosin, 'Christians and Culture: Finding Place in Clio's Mansions,' in *Christ and Culture: The Church in a Post-Christian(?) America*, edited by Robert Rosin (St. Louis: Concordia Seminary Monograph Series, 1995), pp. 57–96. The essay looks at how Christianity has struggled to engage and shape culture while identifying some of the pitfalls of postmodern presuppositions and methods. Like Lowenthal's book in the previous note, in the time since and upon some reconsideration, there is more that could be said along with changes as well. Perhaps the best to add to and qualify the picture is Carl Michalson, *The Hinge of History: An Existential Approach to the Christian Faith* (New York: Charles Scribner Sons, 1959). Michalson makes plain that seeking to sort of facts is one thing, but Christianity also includes promises attached to history or facts, and so there are limits to what can be proved, while a message has to be delivered or proclaimed.

3   Paulo W. Buss, *Integrity and Integration in Ecclesiastical Historiography: The Perspective of Mosheim and Neander* (Unpublished ThD dissertation, Concordia Seminary, St. Louis, 1994). Buss traces the shift (even erosion) that occurs as principles of Reformation theology come under pressure in subsequent ages, each thinking it is being faithful to the essence even as it reshapes basic ideas. Ironically, the historians recording these developments turn out to be the most conservative observers, more so than those in other theological disciplines, although the historians also do not escape pressures of their own context demanding integration of theology on their terms.

Although the integrity and integration terms are not used, the same principle lies behind a volume often used in missiology: Lamin Sanneh, *Translating the Message: The Missionary Impact on Culture* (Maryknoll, NY: Orbis, 1989; revised 2nd ed., 2009). Sanneh argues that over two millennia much of Christianity's success (if that word can be used) has come by learning how to teach, bridge cultures, impart the message, and then let go and get out of the way as the message takes root in different people in new places, who assume the responsibility of proclamation and then start that process again. Despite recognizing a family resemblance across time and place, Christianity does not work like a cookie cutter.

4  The text of the 95 Theses, as they are popularly called, is titled 'Disputatio pro declaratione virtutis indulgentiarum' and is in *Martin Luthers Werke* (Weimar: Böhlau, 1883–), vol. 1, pp. 233–38. (Hereafter cited as WA; thus WA 1, 233–38.)

5  William of Occam, a Franciscan come from England to the University of Paris, came under heavy papal pressure for his criticism of the Avignon papacy's leadership, and small wonder, given Occam's comment that any washwoman had the right to call for a church council. Yet even then the council would not be run by the washwoman or people of her standing but by the episcopal leadership of the church with the papacy presiding but also taking direction from that collected wisdom gathered in sacred assembly.

6  The term comes from Thomas S. Kuhn, *The Structure of Scientific Revolutions*, 2nd ed. (Chicago: University of Chicago Press, 1970). It has become fashionable to apply 'paradigm shift' to every sort of change that seems to be happening in culture today, but Kuhn's original term had a much narrower (and useful) definition. Scientific progress is not by steady, regular, or inevitable as if progress is nearly automatic. Instead, Kuhn argued, the history of science showed periods of no significant development, with plateaus or lulls where little happens and people must be satisfied with the status quo. These periods are interrupted by conscious efforts to upset that status quo when people become dissatisfied with the answers given by the present way of thinking and deliberately work to undo the old and force a drastic rethinking – a paradigm shift. So shifts are not accidents but rather result from disenchantment with the present and an intentional desire to find a new way of viewing reality. That certainly would seem to apply to Luther's criticism of the church and his total reversal of thinking, putting the message ahead of the structure.

7  Karl Holl long ago correctly argued that once Luther began to see the Gospel grasped by faith as the center point of theology—this already in his early Psalms lectures—then the institutional church's status as the dispenser of salvation would have to give way. The structure would not withstand the onslaught. See Holl, 'Die Entstehung Luther's Kirchenbegriff,' *Gesammelte Aufsätze* (Tübingen: J. C. B. Mohr [Paul Siebeck], 1932), vol. 1, pp. 288–325para.

8  Text of 'Disputatio Heidelbergae habita' is in WA 1, 253–74.

9  Text of 'Disputatio Joh. Eccii et Lutheri Lipsiae habita' is in WA 2, 254–383.

10 On Luther's view of church in these pivotal years beginning with 1519 see Carl Axel Aurelius, *Verborgene Kiche: Luthers Kirchenverständnis aufgrund seiner Streitschriften und Exegese 1519–1521* (Hannover: Lutherisches Verlagshaus, 1983).

11 Text of 'An den christlichen Adel deutscher Nation' is in WA 6, 404–69.

12 Luther is consistent in this view that the prince or king is not in the *Predigtamt* when, for example, he lectures later on the Old Testament book of Ecclesiastes. In his opening comments, Luther suggests the book might have better been named 'The Preachings' rather than 'The Preacher' (Der Prediger Salomo) since Solomon, the

presumed source of the wisdom, is not really a preacher but rather is imparting divine wisdom, divine sayings that others then transcribed. There was nothing wrong with providing such wisdom, and Solomon, while offering spiritual leadership to the people, did so as the people's spokesman, not as a priest of Levi.

13  The involvement of secular leaders in ecclesiastical affairs has a long, well-known history. At times matters build to a dramatic head such as in the Investiture Controversy in 1077 with Emperor Henry IV standing penitent in the snow at Canossa awaiting Gregory VII's pardon. But those examples, be they dramatic or only a tempest in a teapot, always presumed there was some sacred calling and authority to be exercised. The question was over who would control it: the church alone or in tandem with secular rulers. Luther wipes away that sacred-secular distinction, though he also maintains the integrity of both the spiritual and secular offices and service in the same.

14  Beyond this first wall, we could go on to talk about the other two, that only popes can call church councils and that only popes ultimately can interpret the Scriptures. But they touch even more on the authority issue, while the first wall also rests on a foundation of church structure.

15  Robert Rosin, 'The Reformation, Humanism, and Education: The Wittenberg Model for Reform,' *Concordia Journal*, 16 (1990): 301–18.

16  WA-Briefwechsel, vol. 1, no. 74 (to Jodokus Trutfetter on May 9, 1518).

17  WA 18, 651–52.

18  WA 6, 301. WA 18, 652. Line 23 says that 'abscondita est ecclesia, latent sancti,' that is, 'the church is hidden, the saints are concealed.'

19  The phrase 'paedestinatorum universitas' is in WA 2, 287. This understanding of the church is like Luther's rejection of popes and councils at Leipzig: they may seem like rash statements but these are not spur-of-the-moment ideas that just pop up. As noted above, Luther had already wondered privately about the pope as antichrist before he lashed out at Leipzig.

20  WA 7, 743. 'Regnum Christi solido simplicique Evangelii verbo regitur.'

21  WA 7, 721. 'Tota vita et substantia Ecclesiae est in verbo dei.'

22  WA 7, 720. '. . . oportet enim aliquod visibile signum dari, quo congregemur in num ad audiendum verbum dei.'

23  WA 7, 720. 'Triae haec sunt Christianorum symbola, tessare et caracteres. . . . In his enim vult nos Christus concordare.'

24  WA 7, 721. 'Non de evangelio scripto sed vocali loquor.' ('I am not talking about the written Gospel but about the spoken.')

25  In fact is might be argued that if the spoken or proclamatory dimension is missing, the mere words printed on the page are not really true theology in terms of engaging

within the church. Being correctly framed in terms of grammar and dogma does not suffice. The word does not stand idle but is used. It is to create and engage. When Erasmus did his Latin translation of the New Testament, he translated logos of John 1 not as *verbum* but as *sermo*. *Verbum* had an active dimension to it, but it also could be a static vocable, while *sermo* has a stronger connotation of a spoken word, the activity of addressing someone. So God does not simply have vocables that sit there in some peaceful abstract or static state. Rather God's speaking is active and creating. So here with Luther and the Gospel, the most important thing is not to settle in on some formulation and then declare that true theology exists (though how things are framed is certainly important). Rather true theology is the word being used. A book title sums this up: Gerhard Forde, *Theology Is for Proclamation* (Minneapolis: Augsburg Fortress, 1990).

26 Murner charged Luther with thinking in terms of a *platonicam civitatem*. As Luther put it, Murner said Luther intended 'ein kirch bawen wie Plato ein statt, die nyndert were,' that is, he wanted to 'build a church like Plato's city that was nowhere.' WA 7, 683. Worth noting is that 'nowhere' is, in Plato's Greek, 'utopia,' not a paradise but a nonexistent state of being. With the Gospel working amid flesh and blood people, that was hardly the case with Luther.

27 WA 40/II, 560. 'Facies ecclesiae est facies peccatricis, vexatate, desertae, morientis et contristate.'

28 The unbroken line tempts us to look for some institutional thread, but that would be shifting the emphasis away from Christ and his work. In WA 30/III, 89, Luther says 'without a doubt there is and will remain a holy Christian church on earth till the end of the world ... [but] this church is nothing other than the believers in Christ who believe and teach ... and are persecuted and martyred in the world because of [the faith]. For where the Gospel is proclaimed and the sacraments used rightly, there the holy Christian church exists, but it is not bound to laws and its splendor is not bound to time and place or to people or appearances.'

29 Apology IV, 5. '... societas externarum rerum ac rituum sicut aliae politiae, sed principaliter est societas fidei et S. S. in cordibus, quae tamen habet externas notas ...'

30 WA 30/III, 561 and 564.

31 Luther's comment is in WA 7, 753. The Christian versus papist distinction is from Lazarus Spengler, a humanist and leader both in city government and in church reform in Nürnberg.

32 The approach is hardly confined to Reformation times. Today it is not difficult to find cases of church organizations that steer clear of solving some theological problem purely in that realm and instead cite bylaws or vote for a procedural resolution. That may bring a quicker end, but what kind of solution really is that? It might be argued that when one has to resort to bylaws, the battle may be won, but the larger war is lost. Early church debates may have run on but one wonders if people were not better off

then rather than after Constantine inserted himself with political interests to complicate theological matters.

33  An interesting reassessment arguing for Luther's catholicity while the Reformation fell to structure is Daniel Olivier, *Luther's Faith: The Cause of the Gospel in the Church*, trans. John Tonkin (St. Louis: Concordia Publishing House, 1982). Olivier argues that Luther's message was catholic, that is, Luther's theology was the sort heard in the history of the church and was not heretical. Olivier illustrates this by using extended quotations from Luther. Nevertheless, because Luther's theology clashed and criticized Rome's perception of what should have been acceptable, Rome refused to consider Luther's view and, after years of trying to deal with its expression on a more individual and particular level, Rome finally dealt with the Reformation at Trent, establishing definitions and then declaring the Reformation outside those definitions. In short, rather than continue a difficult discussion with the Reformation, Trent slammed the door and labeled Reformation theology heretical. In effect, structure triumphed over proclamation. What is particularly interesting about Olivier's book is that the author is a Roman Catholic priest and Reformation historian. As part of what was called 'New Catholic' school of Reformation interpretation (now smaller as proponents retire and die), Olivier argues for reconsidering Luther's theology, especially in the wake of Vatican II, which Olivier believes has opened possibilities.

34  On Luther's older age shift to management with a church on his hands, so to speak, see James M. Kittelson, 'Luther as Church Bureaucrat,' *Concordia Journal*, 13 (1987): 294–306.

35  WA 11, 412.

36  See Luther's comments in WA 10/III, 171, on persons not qualified for the office. And then noting that things are to be done in order (WA 12, 189), and noting that not everyone can speak at once, a person is chosen to fill the office, becoming that congregation's pastor. In WA 10/III, 395, Luther says 'If we were all to preach, it would be like women going to the market. No one would want to listen to the other person and everyone would want to speak.'

37  WA 6, 408. 'For without common consent and command a person cannot take on himself that which is common to all.'

38  WA 11, 408–16. Translation in Luther's Works, 39, 303–14. See Gert Haendler, *Luther on Ministerial Office and Congregational Function*, ed. and trans. Eric C. and Ruth W. Gritsch (Philadelphia: Fortress Press, 1981). Jan Aarts, *Die Lehre Martin Luthers über das Amt der Kirche* (Helsinki: Luther-Agricola Gesellschaft, 1972).

39  So the right to call or place might rest with a city council, with a prince or other royal, with a patron of the congregation, with the people themselves. There are even cases of parents helping to arrange the support for a son to fill a position.

40  Those with a lofty magisterial attitude that clerics are in charge ought to look at WA 15, 721. 'To ordain is not to consecrate. Therefore if we know a godly man, we

bring him forward and by the power of the word that we have we give him the authority to preach the word and give the sacraments. This is ordaining. . . . On the basis of ordination it is established from that election that, for the sake of retaining order, not everyone should have the desire to preach. Thus they have the obligation to perform their ministry, but not perpetually. We can commit it to him today, and tomorrow we can take it away again. The priesthood we have from Christ is perpetual. The other thing is the ministry.' ('Ordinare non est consecrare. Si ergo scimus pium hominem, extrahimus eum et damus in virtute verbi quod habemus, auctoritatem praedicandi verbum et dandi sacramenta. Hoc est ordinare. . . . Ex ordinatione constituitur auss der wal, ut maneat ordo, ne quisque velit praedicare. Item debent ministerium suum agere, sed non perpetuo: possumus ei hodie commendare, cras iterum adimere. Perpetuum est sacerdotium, quod a Christo accepimus. Illud est ministerium.')

**41** Giorgio Agamben, *The Church and the Kingdom*, trans. Leland de la Durantaye (London: Seagull Books, 2012). In contrast to Agamben's ancient image of the church, a very different model is David P. Daniel, 'A Spiritual Condominium: Luther's Views on Priesthood and Ministry with Some Structural Implications,' *Concordia Journal*, 14 (1988): 266–82, a modern take on believers as priests and participants, not by-standers but people with an active interest 'in the building.'

# 5

# The development of Wittenberg ecclesiology

*Robert Kolb*

In the Smalcald Articles Martin Luther defined the church by claiming that 'a seven-year-old child knows what the church is: holy believers and the little sheep who hear the voice of their shepherd. . . . This holiness does not consist of surplices, tonsures, long albs, or other ceremonies of theirs that they have invented over and above the Holy Scriptures. Its holiness exists in the Word of God and true faith.'[1] He was echoing Philip Melanchthon in the Augsburg Confession, article eight, 'the Christian church is, properly speaking, nothing else than the assembly of all believers and saints.'[2] Article seven had already asserted, 'For this is enough for the true unity of the Christian church, that there the gospel is preached harmoniously according to a pure understanding and the sacraments are administered in conformity with the divine Word. It is not necessary for the true unity of the Christian church that uniform ceremonies, instituted by human beings, be observed everywhere.'[3]

Melanchthon's definition chose language similar to the definition of the church in the Code of Justinian that determined for the ancient Roman empire what it meant to be legally a Christian. The coincidence of this legal definition with the theology of the Wittenberg reformers provided a good basis for strengthening Melanchthon's argument that Luther's reforms did not stray outside the bounds of the catholic tradition. That was the goal of the princes and town councils whose confession the Augsburg Confession was. They wished to prevent the emperor from sending military forces to end their reform measures. Noteworthy in both Luther's and Melanchthon's definition is the negative foil of their delineation of what the church is: the church is not determined or defined by its ritual practices or observances.

In his definitive essay on Luther's doctrine of the church David P. Daniel outlines the development of Luther's conception of the church in five stages: 1513–1517, 1518–1521, 1521–1526, 1525/1526–1530, 1530–1546.[4] This essay does not repeat this helpful analysis but presents Luther's concretization of his ideas in practical measures within the context of his understanding of how God gathers his people into the various institutional forms which 'the church' takes. It does not examine the critique of the medieval hierarchical system of church governance and particularly the papacy's role in that system, which played an essential role in Luther's reconstitution of the doctrine and practice of the church.[5] It does not treat Luther's distinction of the 'hidden' and 'revealed' church that aided him in treating the communion of saints in relationship to the institutional forms of the church.[6] Instead, this study offers glimpses of Luther's and Melanchthon's application of their theological foundation for viewing and experiencing the church on the practical level.

Luther's redefinition of the church grew out of his redefinition of what it means to be Christian. He had grown up with a religious system and structure that outwardly bore the marks of the Bible. In fact, it was configured by the rhythms and presuppositions of the pagan religions that had formed the mindsets and worldviews of the original converts of the German tribes over a half millennium earlier. The church that welcomed the conversions of tribal chiefs and area princes in the eighth and ninth centuries did not have sufficient personnel to catechize adequately. The result was a change of names but not of the religious imagination of the population. They perceived the basic structure of contact with the divine in the offerings of good works brought by human beings. They particularly emphasized religious or sacred activities as that which established and preserved the relationship with whatever higher powers there might be. The human performance, particularly of rites, exercises, customs, and usages in the sacred sphere, insured blessings both spiritual and temporal.[7]

The formal dogmatic definition of the church had come in bits and pieces, but an important framework – though negative foil – for thinking about what constituted the church had come in the condemnation of Jan Hus a century earlier by the Council of Constance, which formally rejected a number of his positions on 22 February 1418. The council condemned his definition of the church as the 'totality of the predestined', his rejection of Peter as head of the holy catholic church, his claim that the papal office and its power had grown out of the power of the emperor, and his refusal to believe that divine revelation had made anyone 'part of the church', as the Roman obedience was.[8] Luther's initial rejection of Hus gave way, as he read Hus's writings, to admiration and a recognition that while their doctrines of the church were not precisely the same, they shared many common positions.[9]

Luther's own personality provided the seedbed for his search for a new understanding of the faith; his Ockhamist training at the university supplied the presuppositions. They included Ockham's view of the absoluteness of God's almighty power and his nature as a Creator, who used human language to present himself to sinners. Against this background Luther's immersion in Scripture led him to discover this God who was not waiting for sacred sacrifices from human beings but who instead was coming to them to initiate the relationship. He was addressing them with his expectations for their performance in his law and promising them deliverance from all forms of evil through the work of Christ. God became human, Luther taught at the heart of his message, so that he could be 'handed over [into death] for our sins and raised to restore us to righteousness' (Rom. 4:25). His Word that delivers the benefits of Christ's work, for example in its baptismal form, buries sinful identities and raises his people up as newly-born children of God (Rom. 6:3–11). This action of Christ becomes the orientation for the believer's identity through trusting the promise that bears his saving work: God's restoration of righteousness rests not only on his Word and perception of his chosen people but also on their faith that agrees with God that they have become righteous.[10]

Luther believed that God's conversation with his people goes on through his people. All the baptized have been entrusted with his Word and, as children, they want to imitate their heavenly Father. They cannot suppress the secrets of his love. Above all, God speaks to sinners through those servants of the Word who receive the commission to serve as public ministers to lead the congregation of the faithful into continuous dialogue with the Creator.

This focus on God's Word led inevitably to a change of definition of the church and many aspects of church life while at the same time Luther strove to retain, although often recast, as much of ecclesiastical tradition and practice as could be observed without falling back into the idolatry which haunted medieval Christianity as a constant temptation and trap.

## Luther's identifying 'marks' of the church

There is much more to Luther's understanding of the church than the simple statement of Smalcald Articles. Luther extended his definition when he formulated a description of how to identify the true church by its 'marks' in two later works. The first, *On the Councils and the Church*, was written in 1539 to help prepare for discussions at the papally-called council and for the negotiations which Emperor Charles V had mandated that took place in 1540 and 1541 in Worms and Regensburg. Although Luther was not proposing a dogmatic list of marks in 1539, he repeated and expanded slightly this list in 1541, when he attacked Duke Heinrich of Braunschweig-Wolfenbüttel in his

*Wider Hans Worst.* In this latter work Luther defined the true church not only positively through its marks but also negatively, by identifying the characteristics of the false church as embodied in the Roman obedience. The term 'marks of the church' had been used by medieval theologians but had not become a dogmatic category in their systems, and Luther did not make it such, either.[11] Not intended to set down absolute categories for guiding the church's life, these lists instead reasserted the catholic nature of the Wittenberg churches.

The impact of Luther's redefinition of being Christian, and thus of what the church is took form in the use of God's Word by the Christian congregation and in other aspects of church life. In *On the Councils and the Church* Luther reiterated his complaint, voiced in the Large Catechism,[12] about the foreign word 'church'. No one properly understands 'Kirche', he said, and think of it as a building, whereas 'ecclesia' means 'the people of God'. It is the human creatures chosen by God that constitute the 'holy catholic church', that is, the holy people of Christ. Their holiness is bestowed by the Holy Spirit as he renews heart, soul, body, activity and conduct.[13]

The sanctifying power of the Holy Spirit bestows 'true fear and love for God', with the result that believers 'love, praise, thank, and honor him for all that occurs, good or evil'. He further sanctifies them so that they live in accord with the second table of the law, 'inducing them to obey parents and rulers willingly, to conduct themselves peacefully and humbly, to be not wrathful, vindictive, or malicious, but patient, kind, obliging, brotherly, and loving, not unchaste, not adulterous or lewd, but chaste and pure with wife, child, and servants, or without wife and child.' Luther continued through the commandments, describing the church in terms of the behavior of its members. The holiness of the church consists of its people's trust in God and their reaction to his goodness in their praise of him and their care for his creatures. That the church is holy refers to both the true faith and the faithful life of Christ's people.[14]

Luther then ventured into formulating a list of marks which identify the people who are truly Christ's church. They possess, first of all 'the holy Word of

God', though not all have it in equal measure, according to Saint Paul, in 1 Corinthians 3:12–14. Luther consistently acknowledged that the church embraces more than just the core of faithful confessors; the Holy Spirit has also gathered those who trust in Christ but fail to comprehend some aspects of the biblical message. Nonetheless, he continued, Jesus said that the church is identified by public confession in Matthew 10:32: 'everyone who confesses me before other people I will confess before my Father and the angels.' Christ 'was speaking of the external Word, preached orally by people like you and me, for this is what Christ left behind as an external sign, by which his church, or his Christian people in the world, should be recognized.' This Word as it is 'preached, believed, confessed, and lived' demonstrates the presence of the true church. That Luther was at the same time deconstructing the medieval view of the church defined by its sacred ritual activities and religious rites, as well as vexatious false brethren who also opposed the papacy, is clear as Luther continues, 'This [Word of God] is what performs all miracles, effects, sustains effects, and does everything, exorcises all devils, like pilgrimage-devils, indulgence-devils, bull-devils, brotherhood-devils, saints-devils, mass-devils, purgatory-devils, monastery-devils, priest-devils, rabble-devils, insurrection-devils, heresy-devils, all pope-devils, also Antinomian-devils...'[15] Against them all Luther cited what he claimed Augustine had said, 'The church is begotten, cared for, nourished, and strengthened by God's Word.'[16]

Second, baptism marks the church, as a holy bath of regeneration which sanctifies the people of God. Third, the sacrament of the altar consecrates all of God's people, and its sanctifying power does not depend on those who administer it or those who receive it, a rejection of Donatism. Fourth, God's people are recognized by the office of the keys, the public exercise of forgiveness and the call to repentance. Fifth, the public administration of these oral and sacramental forms of God's Word constitute the office and obligation, the calling, of the servants of the Word.[17]

The people's use of God's Word for praise, prayer, and instruction constitute the sixth mark of the church. The Holy Spirit is sanctifying them through their prayer and praise, through their dwelling on the Creed and the Ten Commandments, that is, through their application of law and gospel. The seventh mark that identifies the church is that it endures 'every misfortune and persecution, all kinds of trials and evil from the devil, the world, and the flesh' – that is from external and internal opposition to God's Word. The people of God experience this in their own 'inward sadness, timidity, fear, outward poverty, contempt, illness, and weakness'. This conforms them to Christ.[18] At the same time Luther warned that the eschatological battle between God and Satan would continue to mark the church's life, individually and institutionally.[19] In that battle good education plays a vital role, Luther noted, as he admonished readers to live out their callings in their daily lives and to prepare their children for doing so also through good schooling.[20] An ecclesiology of the Word demands a fundamental level of understanding. Schools were not the only medium which could deliver understanding, in Luther's estimate, since throughout his lifetime a majority of Germans continued to receive training for daily life at home. But in *On the Councils and the Church* schooling remained Luther's ideal.

These seven marks are, however, not the only marks of the church. 'There are other outward signs that identify the Christian church, namely, those signs whereby the Holy Spirit sanctifies us according to the second table of Moses.' Luther then listed the vices that the Holy Spirit casts out of Christian lives and the virtues that he cultivates. The proper behavior of honorable lives lived in accord with the second table of the law is the result of the sanctifying action of the Holy Spirit, but it is not a sign that in and of itself reveals the existence of the church in so far as these outward works may occur in the lives of those outside the faith as well. But where the Holy Spirit is at work through the Word, Luther believed, such lives will give witness to his presence and love.[21]

Luther's polemic of 1541 against Duke Heinrich of Braunschweig-Wolfenbüttel was provoked by the prince's reputation both as an adulterer and as a defender of the papacy, as well as by his vicious public insults aimed at Luther's elector, Johann Friedrich and his burning down the imperial or free town of Einbeck in an effort to force it back to the Roman obedience and into his own domains. Luther again listed 'marks of the church', although in a slightly different order than found in *On the Councils and the Church*, and with the addition of the walks of life in which Christian love is demonstrated. In asserting that those embracing Wittenberg reforms were part of the church catholic, Luther listed the characteristics that prove that: baptism, the Lord's Supper, the office of the keys, the preaching office and God's publicly proclaimed Word, the confession of the faith in the Apostles Creed, the practice of prayer with the Lord's Prayer (the catechism formed the foundation of Christian knowledge and practice in Luther's view), the honouring of temporal government, the honouring and proper practice of marriage, the suffering imposed by Satan and his minions upon God's people, and the rejection of the use of violence in the service of the church.[22] Here the eighth mark of the church in *On the Councils and the Church* is expressed in terms of the affirmation of the godliness of life in the societal realm and in the family, as well as in the rejection of the use of violent means on behalf of the gospel.

In this treatise Luther offered a deconstruction of the medieval definition of the church. The Roman obedience did not match the biblical definition of the people of God on twelve or more counts. Most had to do with its use of ritual practices as aids to achieving salvation or God's favour. The papal party had deprived baptism of its continuing role in the lives of the baptized by denying that its forgiving power accompanies them their entire lives. It imposed satisfactions upon sinners that led to 'indulgences, pilgrimages, brotherhoods, masses, purgatory, monasteries, convents, and other abominations'. It exalted a pinch of salt and holy water over baptism. It was perverting the Lord's Supper into a sacrifice for sin that takes honour from Christ. It oppressed consciences in the practice of penance. It had replaced good preaching with human teachings and lies. It had imposed a human head upon the church, and he was acting like a temporal ruler though Christ's kingdom is spiritual. It was giving the saints worship due to God alone. It reviled and condemned marriage. It was waging war and shedding innocent blood.[23] Those under the papal obedience, Luther asserted, demonstrated that they did not represent Christ's church by their idolatrous ritual practices and their use of violence.

Luther intended that these marks of the church should identify the people of God at every level of his understanding of 'church', but they certainly applied, he believed, to the place where the people of God experience community with God and with fellow believers most concretely, the local congregation. Within the local congregation individual believers were to count themselves as involved in the larger complex of the worshipping body of Christ in the town or village. Luther's comments in various published works treated three or four levels of the existence of Christ's people in Wittenberg: the local congregation and the territorial church were foundational for the experience of most believers. He also spoke of institutional forms of the church throughout the world, while not a single institution, as 'church'. In addition, although the terminology 'visible' and 'invisible church' became prominent in Lutheran circles only later,[24] he regarded the collection of all the saints of God, living and departed, as Christ's church, not entirely invisible since at least in part it could be apprehended in the use of the Word in audible, tastable, tangible forms. Thus, we can assure members that they are members of the 'invisible' or 'hidden' church if they are faithfully involved in Word in oral, written, and sacramental forms (though full of hypocrites and false teachers – battleground between God and Satan).

The Wittenberg theologians were in no position to make practical provisions for the international church, apart from the deconstruction of papal power, and for the church that embraces all the saints as a whole. They made relatively few provisions for the territorial church although they did mandate the offices of area superintendent and territorial superintendent.[25] These offices were integrated into the administration of the local municipal authorities or the territorial ruler. This implemented Luther's call in 1520 for the princes to exercise episcopal responsibilities 'because of the emergency situation'.[26] It is important to note that in fact the exercise of princely direction and control in ecclesiastical affairs in their lands did not depart significantly from the practices of the late fifteenth century. Following the example of papal claims to absolute power, and the 'catholic and Christian kings' of France and the Iberian principalities, German princes had taken on more and more control of various aspects of society, and their role in ecclesiastical governance was in the forefront of these developments.[27] One major concern driving the organization of the visitation of Saxon congregations in 1527 and 1528 centred on promoting 'the peace of the land', for princes and people of the time recognized that disorder at every level of society was diminishing the quality of life.[28] The reordering of ecclesiastical life certainly served such goals of secular governments as well as the desire of the Wittenberg theologians for the reform of piety and ecclesiastical life according to biblical standards.

## The life of the church in the local congregation

Because for Luther the church arises out of God's Word, the use of his Word by all the baptized permeated the reformer's concept of being a member of the body of Christ. The use of God's Word in the family circle laid the foundation for its use at every level of society.[29] For sixteenth-century thinking, the congregation consisted not only of individuals, who have their own personal relationship with God, but also of family units – parents, children, servants, other relatives – in which the Word of God was present and functioning, for the admonition, comfort, and learning of all. Luther regarded the home as a place in which God wishes his Word to be used first of all, among the members of the family. The rising level of education made devotional reading possible, but quite apart from literate families, those homes in which no one could read could use God's Word through the catechism. Most Lutheran church ordinances required knowledge of the catechism for marriage because the raising of children in the fear, admonition, and knowledge of the Lord belonged to the fundamental purposes of marriage. The translation of the Bible into German was designed to facilitate the practice of devotional meditation in the family. Luther's introductions to sections of the Bible and to some individual books helped parents explain Scripture, as did the marginal notes.[30]

In his *German Mass* of 1526, Luther proposed a model for playful pedagogy with his game of two sacks or purses, one labelled 'faith', the other labelled 'love' – the former for verses which give assurance of God's saving love, the latter for those with the law's instruction of children and servants for daily Christian life. Luther continued, 'Nobody dare regard himself as too clever and dismiss such games for children. When Christ wanted to educate human beings, he became human. If we want to educate children, we have to become children with them. I wish to God that such children's games were widely practiced. Soon we would see a great abundance of Christians and souls prospering in Scriptures and the knowledge of God . . . who daily go to hear a sermon.' Luther observed that church attendance in itself will not insure retention of the message: daily use of the catechism and/or Scripture itself is necessary. 'There is enough written in books. But not everything has been driven home into the heart.'[31]

Luther prescribed use of the core of the catechism, the Ten Commandments, the Apostles Creed, and the Lord's Prayer, for use in the home; in his preface to his Large Catechism he demanded that 'every head of a household at least once week examine the children and servants one after the other to ascertain what they know or have learned of [the basic Christian instruction in the catechism], and if they do not know it, to keep them faithfully at it.'[32] His own routine at home put his ideals into practice, as he reported to those gathered one evening in the Black Cloister for conversation. His son Hans and his daughter Magdalena heard questions such as 'what does it mean when you pray, "Our Father, who art in heaven"?' Luther helped with the answer:

> If I understand these words in faith, that God, who holds heaven and earth in his hands, is my father, I conclude, 'Therefore, I am lord of heaven and earth, Christ is my brother, all things are mine. [The angel] Gabriel is my servant, Raphael is my chauffeur, and all others serve me in all my needs. The Spirit whom my Father in heaven sends me will not let my foot strike against a stone. But this faith does not continue without being attacked. My father moves on and lets me be thrown in jail or lets me drown, and even then we understand these words. Our faith wavers, and our frailty becomes clear. Indeed, who knows if it is really true [we say]. Therefore, this one single word is the most difficult in all of Scripture: "Your" or "our", as in the first commandment, I am your God.'[33]

Luther's student and homiletical biographer Johannes Mathesius experienced such exercises in Melanchthon's home as well. His son, young Philip, prayed the catechism. His daughter Magdalena read from Luther's German catechism, and then others at the table took their turns. One student staying in the home commented on selected proverbs, another on 'sacred history', a third on a paragraph from one of the gospels, a fourth on Livy, a fifth on something Greek – Mathesius thought perhaps Thucydides – a sixth on the Psalms.[34]

Similarly, Luther's friend, Mattthäus Ratzeburger, former court physician for Elector Johann Friedrich the Elder, was undoubtedly unusual in his devotional practice, but according to his pastor, Andreas Poach, Ratzeburger daily read not only passages from medical literature, Galen and Hippocrates, but also from Scripture and Luther's own writings, including the commentaries on the minor prophets, Galatians, Genesis, and selected psalms. Afternoons and evenings at the table he read the German Bible or the appropriate sermons from Luther's *Hauspostille* or *Kirchenpostille* or some other German work of Luther for his wife and children. On Saturday evenings his children and servants heard readings from Luther's Large Catechism, and the housefather heard their recitation of the Small Catechism. Sunday mornings he read passages from the Latin Bible or Luther's commentary on Genesis to his older sons.[35]

Nikolaus von Amsdorf, a friend and sympathizer of Luther, who had been his colleague in Wittenberg before assuming a pastorate in Magdeburg in 1524, tended to be disgruntled and impatient with something less than total faithfulness to Luther's ideals. Thus, it is not surprise that he complained that the reformer's ideal of parental preparation of children for worship and examination of what the young had gained from the sermon was not being implemented anywhere in the German lands. His complaint reflects something of reality in all likelihood, but it also depicts the kind of family life the Wittenberg reformers wished to cultivate.[36]

Beyond the family circle, the Christian congregation took form in the relationship of the members with others in the community, including those estranged from the regular worship life of the congregation. From early in his career as reformer to quite late, Luther emphasized the calling of all believers to share the gospel with one another. Preaching on 1 Peter in 1522, Luther told his listeners that, as followers of Christ, they 'have no other reason for living on earth than to be of help to others. . . . He permits us to live here in order that we may bring others to faith, just as he brought us.'[37] A few weeks later he interpreted Peter's words 'you are a royal priesthood' as simply an explanation of 'you are Christians'. God had called and appointed them as priests, who proclaim God's wonderful deeds that brought them out of darkness into the light and delivered them from all evils. 'Thus you should also teach other people how they, too, come into such light. For you must bend every effort to realize what God has done for you. Then let it be your chief work to proclaim this publicly and to call everyone into the light into which you have been called.'[38]

Their calling as those who speak God's Word to one another arose out of the Lord's commission of his people to speak his Word as it was imposed upon them in their baptism, Luther was convinced. In his postil for the nineteenth Sunday after Trinity, published in 1526, Luther wrote that:

> All who are Christians and have been baptized have this power [to forgive one another's sins]. For with this they praise Christ, and the word is put into their mouth, so that they may and are able to say, if they wish, and as often as it is necessary: 'Look! God offers you his grace, forgives you all your sins. Be comforted; your sins are forgiven. Only believe, and you will surely have forgiveness.' This word of consolation shall not cease among Christians until the last day: 'Your sins are forgiven, be of good cheer.' Such language a Christian always uses and openly declares the forgiveness of sins. For this reason and in this manner a Christian has power to forgive sins.[39]

The Large Catechism reaffirmed the reformer's understanding of what he could label as the 'mutual conversation and consolation' of believers.[40] When 'some particular issue weighs on us or attacks us, eating away at us until we can have no peace' or when we 'find ourselves insufficiently strong in faith', then Luther advised laying one's troubles before another believer 'at any time and as often as we wish'. From fellow Christians believers receive 'advice, comfort, and strength'. For 'by divine ordinance Christ himself has placed absolution in the mouths of his Christian community and commanded us to absolve one another from sins. So, if there is a heart that feels its sin and desires comfort, it has here a sure refuge where it finds and hears God's Word because through a human being God loses and absolves from sin.'[41]

It is clear that he placed formal, public absolution in the mouth of the pastor, but that did not restrict the active application of the gospel to one another by all who belong to Christ. A sermon on John 14:13–14, preached in 1537, Luther reminded the Wittenberg congregation, 'a Christian cannot be still or idle but constantly strives and struggles mightily, as one who has no other object in life than to disseminate God's honor and glory among the people, that others may also receive such a spirit of grace ....'[42] He repeated this instruction to the congregation a few months later in his sermon on Matthew 18:15–20:

> Here Jesus is saying that he does not only want [the condemnation of sin and proclamation of the forgiveness of sins] to take place in the church, but he also gives this right and freedom where two or three are gathered together, so that among them the comfort and the forgiveness of sins may be proclaimed and pronounced. He pours out [his forgiveness] even more richly and places the forgiveness of sins for them in every corner, so that they not only find the forgiveness of sins in the congregation but also at home in their houses, in the fields and gardens, wherever one of them comes to another in search of comfort and deliverance. It shall be at my disposal when I am troubled and sorry, in tribulation and vulnerable, when I need something, at whatever hour and time it may be. There is not always a sermon being given publicly in the church, so when my brother or neighbor comes to me, I am to lay my troubles before my neighbor and ask for comfort .... Again I should comfort others, and say, 'dear friend, dear brother, why don't you lay aside your burdens. It is certainly not God's will that you experience this suffering. God had his Son die for you so that you do not sorrow but rejoice.[43]

Luther's understanding of God's design for humanity did not include, however, anything resembling individualistic modern Western inclinations, and he recognized that God has placed individuals in the network of larger groups, also beyond the family. Regular gathering for worship by a congregation and pastoral leadership and care had a firm place in the reformer's understanding of how God works in the world and what he has intended human life to be. Therefore, Luther did pay attention to the details of congregational life. He did so in a quite unprescriptive way, in contrast not only to the Roman forms of ecclesiastical organization but also to John Calvin's system for organizing and governing the church – although Calvin did concede the validity of an episcopal polity for England instead of the Presbyterian structure he found biblical. In the *German Mass* Luther explicitly stated that his plans need not become standard for churches practicing Wittenberg reforms.[44]

Because God initiated the relationship between himself and his human creatures, and because God loves to converse with his people, Luther deemed 'preaching and teaching of God's Word as 'the most important part of the divine service'[45] and the public absolution of the sins of the worshippers 'the true voice of the gospel announcing remission of sins'.[46] In lecturing on 1 Timothy in 1528, he commented, 'The highest worship of God takes place in preaching the Word since God is worshiped when the gospel is preached, thanks is given, and all the sacrifices and worship of the Old Testament are fulfilled. In this form of worship the neighbor is served and the image of God is formed in people, so that they die and come alive in order to be God-like.' This conversation between God and his people stands at the heart of being human, according to the reformer.[47]

This accentuation of the exposition and application of Scripture in the sermon should not be separated from the sacraments, however. Luther regarded the Lord's Supper as a vital and essential means for the regular delivery of forgiveness of sins, life, and salvation to the people.[48] The system of contacting God through ritual and sacred activities had depended on 'un-Christian fables and lies', which led to making congregational worship 'a work whereby God's grace and salvation might be won'.[49] Luther wished to ground public prayer and praise, like the celebration of the Lord's Supper, on the proclamation of the gospel.[50] For he regarded the human side of the conversation which God initiates as important for the proper expression of what it means to be human.

For a fuller understanding of the foundation of the doctrine of the church which students learned in Wittenberg a study of Philip Melanchthon's concept of the locus 'de ecclesia' is necessary but lies beyond the scope of this investigation. While differing in details at points, Melanchthon's central focus on the Word of God as the constitutive factor and tool of God that assembles his saints both echoed and helped form Luther's own views and played a vital role in the construction of plans for instituting reform in both congregation and territorial church as well as in the Wittenberg call for repentance in the church catholic.[51]

## Concrete plans for the church

The Wittenberg theologians did not only formulate theories about church life. They worked concretely on implementing them. The original intent of the Evangelical princes and towns in composing the Augsburg Confession focused on the justification of specific reforms. Only the attack upon the catholicity of their reform movement led to the first twenty or twenty-one articles treating the teaching of the church. The twenty-first article, on the veneration of the saints, had initially been included among the issues of reform. In fact, article twenty, on faith and good works, deals with the reform of preaching. Along with them, the final seven articles explain and defend the practical decisions made on the basis of the doctrinal articles of the Confession, correcting abuses in the conduct of the Lord's Supper, addressing the dependence on ritual activities, including fasting, clerical celibacy, and monasticism, and the governance of the church by bishops who were distracted by duties as secular rulers.[52]

Even before this attempt to explain the Wittenberg reforms to Emperor Charles V, Luther and Melanchthon, with the help of others, addressed the concrete situation of Saxon congregations in 1528 in their *Instruction for the Visitors* of electoral Saxony. This visitation and the *Instruction* for the visitors were responses to the need to guide local pastors and church leaders in their reforming of congregational life. Luther's postils of 1521 and 1522 had begun his movement in the direction of aiding congregational reform, beginning with the pulpit,[53] and his liturgical works also aimed at making public worship correspond to the new orientation of faith and ecclesiastical life around Scripture. The *Instruction* provides a glimpse into what the Wittenberg reformers regarded as critical for Saxon church life at that time.

Its first article gave pastors instructions on how to distinguish law and gospel, the foundation of the congregation's use of God's Word. The understanding of this framework for good preaching which Luther and Melanchthon and their colleagues were teaching was under challenge from one of the rising stars of the Wittenberg movement at the time, Johann Agricola. His rejection of a role for the law in the Christian life raised concerns with Melanchthon at this time and, a decade later, Luther as well.[54]

The *Instruction* highlighted the core of the medieval catechism that would in the wake of the visitation become the core of Evangelical instruction in the faith. The Creed presumably stands behind the proclamation of the gospel as treated in the first article of the *Instruction*. The gospel is also treated in instructions for giving comfort in times of temptation and trouble, a reflection of one element of Luther's theology of the cross. Special treatment was given cultivation of the use the Ten Commandments and the Lord's Prayer in the life of parish and parishioner. The practice of the sacraments provided a key element of the ways in which God's Word was conveyed in a semi-literate society and important, visible aspects of departure from medieval ritual-centred piety. An article on 'the Ordinances of the Church' offered guidance in the proper use of the customs and pious practices.[55] A biblical understanding of marriage served as the foundation for a well-functioning society. This article, too, countered medieval views that tended to diminish the godliness of the married life while experimenting with formulations for evangelical rules for family life.[56] Articles on 'free will' and 'Christian freedom' addressed facets of the 'antinomian' concerns raised by Agricola as well, as did the distinction of civil and ecclesiastical realms in the article on 'the Turk'.[57] Finally, the *Instruction* contained extensive detail regarding the necessity of schooling and its curricular form. Literacy had become more important than it had ever been in the German lands with the necessity of universal engagement with Scripture in order that God's Word might act in the lives of all.

That the Wittenberg leadership did not intend the *Instruction* to lay down canon law for Evangelical churches is clear from Luther's own refusal to let his plans, for instance, for the form and conduct of the liturgy, become the standard for all territorial and municipal liturgies, and by the reworking of the plan and the publication of an official 'Church Ordinance' for the town of Wittenberg in 1533. It established the office of superintendent for electoral Saxony in Wittenberg, in the person of the pastor of the town church. It treated the duties of the pastor and the deacons of the congregation, chiefly concerned with the preaching and conduct of services throughout the week. Furthermore, regulations concerning the chanting by the school choir and the celebration of the Lord's Supper were formulated. Provisions for the girls school and the Latin school for boys; the three 'hospitals' for the seriously ill and dying; other social welfare support for the poor; and the administration of these activities by elders were stipulated. The payment of the clergy and the manner in which pastors, deacons, and teachers were to be chosen also were specified.[58]

Johannes Bugenhagen carried these concepts of congregational life with him as he answered calls from Denmark, Pomerania, and a number of towns in northern Germany to aid their leadership in introducing reform and establishing an evangelical form for the life of the church. His model for ecclesiastical practice was modified in response to the specific needs of different localities.[59]

# Convictions and concessions in Wittenberg thinking on ecclesiastical life

In addition to such plans for church life that the Wittenberg theologians intended for the governance of church life, they made proposals for the basis of unity with other Christians that addressed issues of practice. In both polity and ritual practice, Wittenberg displayed flexibility in such matters while insisting on the abolition of certain medieval practices and the centrality of justification by grace through faith alone in Jesus Christ. The governments linked in the Smalcald League hoped for at least an informal alliance with both King Francis I of France and King Henry VIII of England in the mid-1530s, and to that end Melanchthon drafted paraphrases of the Augsburg Confession as a doctrinal basis for such alliances. His *Consilium ad Gallos* of 1534 allowed for the retention of the papal and episcopal governance of the church on the condition that those with authority permitted the free preaching of the gospel. For Melanchthon the gospel included the doctrine of justification, the rejection of the understanding of the mass as a sacrifice for sin and communion in only one kind, the rejection of the veneration of saints, monastic vows, and clerical celibacy (although that topic could be left to the decision of a council). He also briefly outlined proper biblical teaching on the freedom of the will, original sin, the free forgiveness of sins, and the necessity of good works. Other matters were to be regarded as adiaphora, and reasonable decisions could be made in regard to them.

Two years later, in 1536, negotiations with representatives of the English court were progressing, and the princes asked Melanchthon to draft a common doctrinal agreement. Sensitive to King Henry's inclinations, which he knew well through the English emissary Robert Barnes, who had studied at Wittenberg, Melanchthon used the language of the Apology of the Augsburg Confession regarding the mass as a eucharistic sacrifice while explicitly rejecting its use as an alleged sacrifice for sin, extending what Christ had done on the cross.[60] He left questions of communion in one kind and clerical celibacy more open than he had in the Augsburg Confession and even in the *Concilium ad Gallos*. As in the previous paraphrase of 1534, monasteries were praised for their potential as schools while compulsory monastic vows for life were criticized. Both documents refused to yield at all on justification of sinners through faith in Christ's atoning work, but the ideals of pious practice expressed in documents for consumption at home were not in every area beyond the German-speaking lands necessary.[61]

The Wittenberg 'Reformatio' of 1545 resembles these negotiating tools with foreign powers more than it does the regulations set in place for Saxony or the principalities and towns provided with Church Ordinances by Johannes Bugenhagen. This document responded to a request from Emperor Charles V, one last attempt to solve the religious problem of his realm before he resorted to military action, which actually came about in 1546 with the outbreak of the Smalcald War. Melanchthon composed this description of ecclesiastical life and the other four members of the faculty, Luther, Johannes Bugenhagen, Georg Major, and Caspar Cruciger, joined Melanchthon in signing it. The Reformatio is less a concrete plan intended for implementation as a negotiating tool aimed at securing peace and protection from imperial violence. Nonetheless, it indicates the concerns that governed the Wittenberg sense of what form the church should take.

Proper church governance requires 'proper pure teaching', which in this 'Reformatio' focuses on the affirmation of creedal Trinitarian and Christological teaching as well as the understanding of justification by grace through faith in Christ. Furthermore, this governance requires 'the proper use of the sacraments;' 'the preaching office and obedience to the pastor as Seelsorger, who conducts the "ministry of the gospel"'. Furthermore, the church needs 'the preservation of proper discipline' by ecclesiastical courts or some other form of spiritual jurisdiction, the preservation of schooling, and the support of pastors in regard to their income and physical needs.[62] Melanchthon made clear the Wittenberg rejection of medieval abuses of confession and absolution, the Lord's Supper (including withholding of the chalice from the laity and regarding the consecration as a supplementary sacrifice to Christ's death for actual sins), the idolatrous practice of the invocation of the saints, and clerical celibacy.[63] The pastoral office was described in terms of the preaching of repentance, the pronouncement of the forgiveness of sins, and proper pastoral care.[64]

These attempts to frame a Wittenberg image of the life of the church in order to preserve peace and stave off military action should not be seen as prescriptive or dogmatic characterizations of an ideal but rather as negotiating tools that do set a boundary of what might be tolerated in order to avoid violent suppression of Wittenberg reform. Nonetheless, they do accentuate the Wittenberg understanding that the proclamation of justification by faith in Christ stands at the heart of life of the church.

## The practice of proclamation in Wittenberg reform

Alongside the development of formal sets of regulations for church life, Luther's ecclesiology of the Word was making its impact. Already in the 1520s demands on and expectations of the priests who were becoming pastors were changing. Not only were ministers of the Word expected to preach for two or three services each Sunday and on festival days. Within the next decade the sermon became an integral part of weddings and funerals, in contrast to medieval practice. This illustrates how Luther's redefinition of being Christian significantly altered various parts of the church's life. When a person died in the late medieval church, the body, of course, had to be disposed of quickly, normally within twenty-four hours, for hygienic reasons. The actual burial had little need for priests, so often the family and neighbours assembled at an appointed hour and carried the body to the cemetery, accompanied by the parish sexton and the boys' choir from the school, singing dirges which mourned the departed. After burial began the never-ending series of masses for the dead that the family could employ to win remission from temporal punishment in purgatory for the deceased. Almost immediately with the introduction of Wittenberg reform, this changed. Burial proceeded according to the same schedule, but the hymns sung on the way to the cemetery celebrated Christ's resurrection, the forgiveness of sin, and the promise of life everlasting and reunion with the loved ones left behind in heaven. Sextons read Bible passages of hope and thanksgiving rather than those of judgment and sorrow at the graveside. After Luther published his funeral sermons for Elector Frederick the Wise in 1525 and Elector Johann in 1532, the funeral sermon that had already begun to be suggested, if not prescribed, in new church orders, slowly became standard fare. Those preached for the nobility and princes, and a bit later for more prominent burgher, were published, as memorials that functioned as devotional reading for families.[65] The great spectrum of passages chosen by parish pastors for their sermons reflects both the extensive knowledge of Scripture which they possessed and their ability to join parishioner and passage together with sensitivity to the situation of the deceased.[66] Nothing important in life or in death could be left alone and apart from God's Word.[67]

Weddings likewise had not commanded the attention of the priest necessarily. The civil/sacred transaction which joined wife and husband took place in front of the church, at the bridal portal oftentimes, or at home. Luther's publication of wedding sermons undoubtedly aided the rising acceptance of the natural and necessary inclusion of words from Scripture in the wedding service.

Education for the pastoral office quickly changed as it reflected this new definition of the church gathered around God's Word. Luther's failure to include lectures on Peter Lombard's *Sententiae* along with his biblical lectures produced a new understanding of the preparation of parish clergy was beginning to take form. With the arrival of Melanchthon in Wittenberg in August 1518, the demand for curricular change took concrete form. His inaugural address called for radical change not only in the liberal arts curriculum but also in the theological faculty:

Regarding theology, it is of utmost importance how they [students of theology] equip themselves for their study. For more than all other areas of study, theology really demands the highest possible capacity for thinking, for intensive concentration, and for precision in analysis. The fragrance of the incense of the Lord is sweeter than the aromatic spices of human fields of learning. Led by the Holy Spirit, accompanied by our education in the arts and sciences, it is possible for us to find access to that which is sacred ... Since the writings that form the basis of theology are written some in Hebrew, some in Greek, we must learn the foreign languages, so that we do not have to meet the theologians like 'masks unable to speak'. First, with the original text we will have access to the words with their luster and their true significance, and, to use a figure of speech, the true and real meaning of the letters, which we are seeking, will reveal itself to us in the glorious light of the midday sun.[68]

Quickly the medieval curriculum receded, to be replaced with lectures on biblical books, changes that were incorporated into the formal adoption of a new curriculum by the theological faculty in 1533. Its core prescribed lectures on the epistle to the Romans, John's gospel, the Psalms, Genesis, and Isaiah, as well as lectures on Augustine's De spiritu et littera.[69] The actual offerings of lectures extended beyond this core, in Wittenberg and other universities influenced by its model. Melanchthon himself delighted in studying Colossians with the students and also offered them his insights into other books as well over the years.[70] His students who became professors also lectured on a spectrum of biblical books although the Wittenberg core remained predominant in the curricula of Lutheran universities.[71]

\* \* \*

Practical matters often dominate discussions of the life and also of the doctrine of the church. Other traditions have developed much more elaborate loci on the church than did the first Lutherans because these other groups tended to dogmatize more elements of the practical issues, due to their perception of the Christian church in terms of polity. Luther focus on the biblical narrative and the teaching derived from it have enabled Lutherans to practice more freedom in regulating expressions of the faith in ritual and polity. Certain situations in Lutheran history have demanded that church leaders formulate specific plans for polity and policy that do not follow the Wittenberg pattern. Luther made allowance for a good deal of variance in the appearance and procedures of contemporary territorial and municipal churches. In David Daniel's words, 'Luther's ecclesiological concern was to define what and where the true church is and to encourage Christians, individually and collectively, to live transformed by the gospel for one another as the body of Christ in this world.'[72] For him and for Melanchthon the church must be viewed as God's chosen people, assembled to receive God's Word, in oral, written, and sacramental forms, and that the use of these forms at every level of the church remain faithful to what is found in Scripture. His ecclesiology rested upon and expressed itself in the church's use of the Word of God.

# Notes

1   *Die Bekenntnisschrfiten der Evangelische-Lutherischen Kirche*, ed. Irene Dingel (Göttingen: Vandenhoeck & Ruprecht, 2014 [henceforth BSELK]), 776/777, 3–11, *The Book of Concord*, ed. Robert Kolb and Timothy J. Wengert (Minneapolis: Fortress, 2000 [henceforth BC]), 4–325. For a insightful overview of the topic and an excellent bibliography, see David P. Daniel, 'Luther on the Church,' in *The Oxford Handbook of Martin Luther's Theology*, ed. Robert Kolb, Irene Dingel and Lubomir Batka (Oxford: Oxford University Press, 2014), 333–352.

2   BSELK 102/103,18–26, BC 42/43.

3   BSELK 102/103, 6–17, BC42/43.

4   Daniel, 'Luther on the Church.'

5   Cf. Scott H. Hendrix, *Luther and the Papacy. Stages in a Reformation Conflict* (Philadelphia: Fortress, 1981).

6    Carl Axel Aurelius, *Verborgene Kirche, Luther's Kirchenverständnis in Streitschriften und Exegesie and 1519-1521* (Hannover: Lutherisches Verlagshaus, 1983).

7    Scott Hendrix, *Recultivating the Vineyard, The Reformation Agendas of Christianization* (Louisville/London: Westminster John Knox, 2004), 1–29.

8    Heinrich Denzinger, ed. *Kompendium der Glaubensbekenntnisse und kirchliche Lehrentscheidungen*, ed. Peter Hünermann (Freiburg/Breisgau: Herder, 1991), 438–443.

9    Martin Wernisch, 'Luther and Medieval Reform Movements, Particularly the Hussites,' in *Oxford Handbook*, 62-70, and Philip N. Haberkern, *Patron Saint and Prophet: Jan Hus in the Bohemian and German Reformations* (Oxford/New York: Oxford University Press, 2016).

10   Robert Kolb, 'Resurrection and Justification. Luther's Use of Romans 4,25,' *Lutherjahrbuch* 78 (2011), 39–60.

11   Gordon Lathrop and Timothy J. Wengert, *Christian Assembly: Marks of the Church in a Pluralistic Age* (Minneapolis: Fortress, 2004), 54–56.

12   BSELK 1030/1031, 34–1034/1035,14, BC 436–438.

13   WA 50:625, 3–626, 15, LW41: 144–145.

14   WA 50: 626, 16–628, 28, LW 41: 146–147.

15   WA 50: 628, 29–630, 8, LW 41: 148–150.

16   WA 50: 630, 16–20, LW 41: 151.

17   WA 50: 630, 21–633, 24, LW 41: 151–154.

18   WA 50: 641, 20–643, 5, LW 41: 164–165.

19   WA 50: 644, 12–649, 29, LW 41: 167–171.

20   WA 50:651, 15–652, 17, LW 41: 176–178.

21   WA 50: 652, 18–653, 15, LW 41: 166–167.

22   WA 51: 479, 4–485, 24, LW 41: 194–198.

23   WA 50: 487, 29–499, 20, LW 41: 199–205.

24   Kenneth G. Appold, *Orthodoxie als Konsensbildung. Das theologische Disputationswesen an der Universität Wittenberg zwischen 1570 und 1710* (Tübingen: Mohr Siebeck, 2004), 173–176, 180–192, 267–270.

25   *Die evangelische n Kirchordnungen des XVI. Jahrhunderts*, ed. Emil Sehling, 1,1 (Leipzig, 1902, Aalen: Scientia, 1979), 700.

26   Cf. Luther's argument in his *Open Letter to the German Nobility*, 1520, WA 6: 407, 33–411,7, LW 44: 124–133.

27  Eike Wolgast, 'Die Einführung der Reformation in den deutschen Territorien zwischen 1525/26 und 1568,' in *Der 'Unterricht der Visitatoren' und die Durchsetzung der Reformation in Kursachsen*, ed. Joachim Bauer and Stefan Michel (Leipzig: Evangelische Verlagsanstalt, 2017), 11–34.

28  Sigrid Westphal, 'Ist der ‚Unterricht der Visitatoren' ein Instrument des landesherrlichen Kirchenregiments?,' in *'Unterricht der Visitatoren'*, 151–164.

29  The reformer regarded the family as the foundation of all societal activities; see his Large Catechism, Fourth Commandment, BSELK 96/9698,11–13, 974/975, 23–976/977, 7, BC 400, 403–404.

30  Robert Kolb, *Martin Luther and the Enduring Word of God. The Wittenberg School and its Scripture-Centered Proclamation* (Grand Rapids: Baker Academic, 2016), 216–230.

31  WA19:78,12–24, LW53:67.

32  BSELK 912/913, 13–15, BC 383.

33  WATR1 31, §81. Taken from Kolb, *Luther and the Enduring Word*, 233–234.

34  WATR5:32, §5257. Cf. Kolb, *Luther and the Enduring Word of God*, 234.

35  *Vom Christlichen Abschied aus diesem sterblichen Leben des lieben thewren Mannes Matthei Ratzenbergers der Artzney Doctors Bericht durch Andream Poach Pfarherrn zun Augustinern in Erffurdt/ vnd andere/ So dabey gewesen/ kurtz zusamen gezogen* (Jena, 1559), A2b-A3a.

36  Robert Kolb, 'Parents Should Explain the Sermon, Nikolaus von Amsdorf on the Role of the Christian Parent,' *The Lutheran Quarterly* o.s. 25 (1973): 231–240.

37  WA 12: 267, 3–7, LW 30:11.

38  WA 12: 318, 26–319, 6, LW 30: 64–65.

39  WA 10, 1:412–414 *Sermons of Martin Luther*, ed. John Nicholas Lenker 5 (1905; Grand Rapids: Baker, 1983), 209.

40  This phrase Luther borrowed from medieval usage in his Smalcald Articles, in treating the means of grace, SA III,iv; BSELK 766/767. 4–5, BC 319.

41  Large Catechism, BSELK, 1159, 33–39, BC 477–478.

42  'Sermons on John 14,' 1537, WA 45: 540, 14–23, LW 24: 87–88. Cf. 'The Sacrament of the Body and Blood of Christ – Against the Fanatics,' 1526, WA 19: 482–523, LW 36: 359.

43  'Sermons on Matthew 18–24,' 1539–1540, WA 47: 297, 36–298,14.

44  WA19: 72, 1–32 , LW 53: 61.

45  *The German Mass* WA19:78, 26–27, LW53: 68. Cf. *Luther and the Enduring Word*, 174–179.

**46**  *An Order of Mass and Communion*, 1523, WA 12:213, 9–11, LW53: 28.

**47**  WA 26:110, 15, LW 28: 369.

**48**  WA12: 206, 15–209,10, LW53: 20–23.

**49**  *Concerning the Order of Public Worship*, 1523, WA12:35, 15–16, LW53: 11.

**50**  *On the Councils and the Church*, WA50:641, 20–34, LW41: 164.

**51**  Cf. Apology of the Augsburg Confession, BSELK 398–423, BC 174–183; and his *Loci communes*, in *Melanchthons Werke in Auswahl* [Studien-Ausgabe], ed. Robert Stupperich 2,2 (Gütersloh: Bertelsmann, 1953): 474–497; Philip Melanchthon: *Corpus Reformatorum. Philippi Melanthonis Opera quae supersunt omnia*, ed. C. G. Bretschneider and H. E. Bindweil (Halle/Braunschweig: Schwetschke, 1834-1860), 21: 505–510 (2. Aetas), 21: 825–847 (3. Aetas), 22: 527–536 (German translation, 3. Aetas).

**52**  Charles P. Arand, James A. Nestingen, Robert Kolb, *The Lutheran Confessions, History and Theology of the Book of Concord* (Minneapolis: Fortress, 2012), 97–104.

**53**  Kolb, *Luther and the Enduring Word*, 191–195.

**54**  Cf. Timothy J. Wengert, *Law and Gospel, Philip Melanchthon's Debate with John Agricola of Eisleben over Poenitentia* (Grand Rapids: Baker, 1997), 77–210; Joachim Rogge, *Johann Agricolas Lutherverständnis* (Berlin: Evangelische Verlagsanstalt, 1960), Steffan Kjellgaard-Pedersen, *Gesetz, Evangelium und Busse: Theologiegeschichtliche Studien zum Verhältnis zwischen dem jungen Johann Agricola (Eisleben) und Martin Luther* (Leiden: Brill, 1983); Ernst Koch, 'Johann Agricola neben Luther: Schülerschaft und theologische Eigenart,' in *Lutheriana*, ed. Gerhard Hammer and Karl-Heinz zur Mühlen (Cologne: Böhlau, 1984), 131–150. Cf. Also Ernst Koch, 'Die Bedeutung von Gesetz und Evangelium nach dem 'Unterricht der Visitatoren,'' in *'Unterricht der Visitatoren,'* 195–212.

**55**  Volker Leppin, 'Die Normierung der Frömmigkeit im 'Unterricht der Visitatoren'', in *'Unterricht der Visitatoren,'* 167–194.

**56**  Rals Frassek, 'Die eherechtlichen Passagen des 'Unterricht der Visitatoren' im Kontext des frühen evangelischen Eherechts,' in *'Unterricht der Visitatoren,'* 213–240.

**57**  Michael Beyer, 'Hintergründe der Lehre vom ‚freien Willen' und der, christlichen Freiheit 'im Unterricht der Visitatoren' in *'Unterricht der Visitatoren,'* 241–255; Johannes Ehmann, 'Der Artikel vom Türken im ‚Unterricht der Visitatoren', in *'Unterricht der Visitatoren,'* 255–264.

**58**  *Die evangelische n Kirchordnungen*, 1,1, 700–710.

**59**  Cf. Thomas Bergholz, 'Reich Gottes und Kirchenordnung. Johannes Bugenhagens kirchen ordnendes Wirken als Ausdruck seiner Ekklesiologie und Zwei-Reiche-Lehre,' in *Der späte Bugenhagen*, ed. Irene Dingel und Stefan Rhein (Leipzig: Evangelische Verlagsanstalt, 2011), 139–150; Among other studies, Heiner Lück, 'Prudentia legislatoria: Regelungssystematik und Regelungstechnik in den Kirchenordnungen Johannes Bugenhagens,' in *Johannes Bugenhagen (1485-1558). Der Bischof der*

*Reformation*, ed. Irmfried Garbe and Heinrich Kröger (Leipzig: Evangelische Verlagsanstalt, 2010), 171–189; Hans-Günter Leder, 'Die reformatorische Ordnuing der Kirche im Herzogtum Pommern . . .,' and 'Bugenhagens reformatorisches Wirken in Dänemark,' *Johannes Bugenhagen Pomeranus—Vom Refomrer zum Reformator*, ed. Volker Gummelt (Frankfurt/M: Lang, 2002), 317–408.

60  BSELK 622/623,7–644/645, 20, BC 260–269.

61  Irene Dingel, 'Melanchthon's Paraphrases of the Augsburg Confession, 1534 and 1536, in the Service of the Smalcald League,' in Irene Dingel, et al., *Philip Melanchthon. Theologian in Classroom, Confession, and Controversy* (Göttingen: Vandenhoeck & Ruprecht, 2012), 104–122.

62  *Melanchthons Briefwechsel*, ed. Heinz Scheible et al., *Texte* 14 (Stuttgart-Bad Cannstatt: fromann-holzboog, 2014 [hencetorth MBWT]): 53–54 (German), 79–80 (Latin); ET: *The Wittenberg Reformation (1545)*, trans. John R. Stephenson (Saint Catherines: Concordia Lutheran Theological Seminary, 2016), 7.

63  MBWT 14: 58–67, 84–93, *Wittenberg Reformation*, 14–23.

64  MBWT 14: 67–74, 93–, *Wittenberg Reformation*, 23–32.

65  Irene Dingel, '"True Faith, Christian Living, and a Blessed Death": Sixteenth Century Funeral Sermons as Evangelical Proclamation,' *Lutheran Quarterly* 27 (2013), 399–420; Cornelia Niekus-Moore, *Patterned Lives: The Lutheran Funeral Biography in Early Modern Germany* (Wiesbaden: Harrasowitz, 2006).

66  Robert Kolb, '[. . .] da jr nicht trawrig seid wie die anderen, die keine hoffnung haben. Der Gebrauch der Heiligen Schrift in Leichenpredigten der Wittenberger Reformation (1560-1600),' in *Leichenpredigten als Medien der Erinnerungskultur im europäischen Kontext*, ed. Eva-Maria Dickhaut (Stuttgart: Steiner, 2014), 1–25.

67  Robert Kolb, 'Orders for Burial in the Sixteenth Century Wittenberg Circle,' in Irene Dingel and Armin Kohnle (ed.), *Gute Ordnung. Ordnungsmodelle und Ordnungsvorstellungen in der Reformationszeit* (Leipzig: Evangelische Verlagsanstalt, 2014), 257–279.

68  *Melanchthons Werke in Auswahl [Studienausgabe]*, ed. Robert Stupperich (E7 vols., Gütersloh: Gerd Mohn, 1951-1975), 3:40, *Melanchthon deutsch, Bd 1. Schule und Universität, Philosophie, Geschichte, und Politik* ed. Michael Beyer, Stefan Rhein, Günter Wartenberg. (Leipzig: Evangelische Verlagsanstalt.Melanchthon: 1997), 57–60.

69  Walther Friedensburg, ed., *Urkundenbuch der Universität Wittenberg. Volume 1* (Magdeburg: Historische Kommission, 1926), 1: 155.

70  Timothy J. Wengert, 'The Biblical Commentaries of Philip Melanchthon,' in Dingel et al. *Melanchthon, Theologian*, 43–76.

71  Kolb, Luther and the Enduring Word, 311–394.

72  Daniel, 'Luther on the Church,' 349.

# 6

# Towards a materialist conspiracy of faith

*Slavoj Žižek*

Those who follow obscure spiritual-cosmological speculations have almost certainly heard of one of the most popular topics in this domain: when three planets (usually Earth, its moon and the sun) find themselves along the same axis, some big cataclysmic event takes place, and the whole order of the universe is momentarily thrown out of joint and has to restore its balance (as it was supposed to happen in 2012). Does something like this not hold for the year 2017 which was a triple anniversary: in 2017, we did not just celebrate the centenary of the October Revolution but also the 150th anniversary of the first edition of Marx's Capital (1867), and the 50th anniversary of the so-called Shanghai Commune when, in the climactic moment of the Cultural Revolution, residents of Shanghai decided to follow literally Mao's call and directly took over the power, overthrowing the rule of the Communist Party (which is why Mao quickly decided to restore order by sending the army to squash the Commune). Do these three events not mark the three stages of the Communist movement: Marx's Capital outlined the theoretical foundations of the Communist revolution, the October Revolution was the first successful attempt to overthrow bourgeois state and build a new social and economic order, while the Shanghai Commune stands for the most radical attempt to immediately realize the most daring aspect of the Communist vision, the abolishment of the state power and the imposition of direct people's power organized as a network of local communes... So what went wrong with this cycle? Perhaps, the answer is to be sought in the fourth anniversary: 2017 was also the 500-year anniversary of 1517 when Martin Luther made public his 95 theses.

Jesus said that a good tree does not bring forth evil fruit (i.e., a good tree produces only good fruit), and Luther concluded from it that 'good works do not make a good man, but a good man does good works'. One should fully assume the 'static' anti-performative (or anti-Pascalean) aspect of this conclusion: we do not create ourselves through the meanders of our life-practice, in our creativity we rather bring out what we already are. It's not 'act as if you are good, do good works, and you will become good', it is 'only if you are good you can do good works'. The easy way to read this claim is to interpret it as a 'necessary illusion': what I am is effectively created through my activity, there is no pre-existing essence or essential identity which is expressed/actualized in my acts; however, we spontaneously (mis)perceive our acts as merely expressing/actualizing what we (already) are in ourselves. However, from a properly dialectical standpoint, it is not enough to say that the pre-existing self-identity is a necessary illusion; we have here a more complex mechanism of (re)creating the eternal identity itself. Let's clarify this mechanism with an example. When something crucial happens, even if it happens unexpectedly, we often get the impression that it had to happen, that it would violate some higher order if it were not to happen. More precisely, once it does happen, we see that it had to happen – but it may not have happened. Let's take a case of desperate love: I am deeply convinced that my love is not reciprocated, and I silently resign myself to a gloomy future of despair; but if I all of a sudden discover that my love is reciprocated, I feel that this had to happen and I cannot even image the despair of my life without it. Or let's take a difficult and risky political decision: although we sympathize with it, we are sceptical, we don't trust the scared majority; but when, as if by a miracle, this decision is taken and enacted, we feel it was destined to happen. Authentic political acts take place like this: in them, (what was considered) 'impossible' happens and, by way of happening, it rewrites its own past and emerges as necessary, 'predestined' even. This is why there is no incompatibility between Predestination and our free acts. Luther saw clearly how the (Catholic) idea that our redemption depends on our acts introduces a dimension of bargaining into ethics: good deeds are not done out of duty but in order to gain salvation. If, however, my salvation is predestined, this means that my fate is already decided and my doing good deeds does not serve anything – so if I do them, it is out of pure duty, a really altruistic act:

> This recognition that only as one was freed from the paralyzing need to serve one's own self, could acts of love become altruistic, was one of Luther's most positive contributions to Christian social ethics. It enabled him to view good deeds as ends in themselves, and never as a means of salvation. /.../ Luther realized that a love that sought no reward was more willing to serve the helpless, the powerless, the poor, and the oppressed, since their cause offered the least prospect of personal gain.[1]

But did Luther draw all ethico-political consequences from this key insight? His great pupil and opponent Thomas Muntzer accused Luther of betrayal: his basic reproach to Luther's social ethics concerns the 'perverse application of the Law-gospel distinction'. The rightful use of the law was to bring 'destruction and sickness to the healthy', and that of the Gospel to bring 'comfort to the troubled'. Luther had turned this application on its head by defending the presumptuous and tyrannical rulers with the gracious words of the Gospel, while bringing the 'grim sternness' of the law to bear against the God-fearing poor and oppressed peasants. The result was a total misuse of Scripture. 'Thus the godless tyrant says to the pious, "I must torture you. Christ also suffered.

Therefore you are not to resist me." [Matthew 5] This [is] a great perversion /.../ one must forgive with the Gospel and the Spirit of Christ, to the furtherance and not the hindrance of the Gospel.'

With this perversion, 'the elect were no longer envisioned as directly active or forceful instruments of that retribution' against those who violate the spirit of the Gospel – this critique of Luther is clear, but it nonetheless seems to court the danger of succumbing itself to the perverse position of perceiving oneself as the direct instrument of big Other's will. How to avoid this danger? Let us begin at the beginning, with the triad of Orthodoxy, Catholicism and Protestantism.

Central to the Orthodox tradition is the notion of 'theosis', of man becoming (like) god, or, to quote Saint Athanasius of Alexandria: 'He was incarnate that we might be made god.' What would otherwise seem absurd – that fallen, sinful man may become holy as God is holy – has been made possible through Jesus Christ, who is God incarnate. St. Maximus the Confessor wrote: 'A sure warrant for looking forward with hope to deification of human nature is provided by the Incarnation of God, which makes man God to the same degree as God Himself became man /.../. Let us become the image of the one whole God, bearing nothing earthly in ourselves, so that we may consort with God and become gods, receiving from God our existence as gods.'[2] This orthodox formula 'God became man so that man can become God' is totally wrong: God became man AND THAT'S IT, nothing more, everything already happens here, what needs to be added is just a new perspective on this. There is no resurrection to follow, Holy Ghost already IS resurrection. Only Protestantism enables us to think Incarnation as an event in God himself, as HIS profound transformation: He was incarnate that HE became God, i.e., He became fully God only through His self-division into God and man. This may sound paradoxical since God is an unknown Beyond, deus absconditus. We thus seems to have three incompatible positions: God is an absolutely impenetrable Beyond; God is the absolute Master of our fate which is predestined by Him; God gave us freedom and thereby made us responsible for our deeds. The unique achievement of Protestantism is to bring together these three positions: everything is predestined by God, but since God is an impenetrable Beyond for me I cannot discern what my fate is, so I am left to do good deeds without any calculation and profit in view, i.e., in total freedom . . .

True freedom is not a freedom of choice made from a safe distance, like choosing between a strawberry cake or a chocolate cake; true freedom overlaps with necessity, one makes a truly free choice when one's choice puts at stake one's very existence – one does it because one simply 'cannot do it otherwise'. When one's country is under a foreign occupation and one is called by a resistance leader to join the fight against the occupiers, the reason given is not 'you are free to choose', but: 'Can't you see that this is the only thing you can do if you want to retain your dignity?' This is why radical acts of freedom are possible only under the condition of predestination: in predestination, we know we are predestined, but we don't know how we are predestined, i.e., which of our choices is predetermined, and this terrifying situation where we have to decide what to do, knowing that our decision is decided in advance, is perhaps the only case of real freedom, of the unbearable burden of a really free choice – we know that what we will do is predestined, but we still have to take a risk and subjectively choose what is predestined.

We cannot escape from the clutches of Fate, but we also cannot escape from the burden of responsibility into Fate. Is this not why psychoanalysis is exemplary of our predicament? Yes, we are decentred, caught in a foreign cobweb, overdetermined by unconscious mechanisms, yes, I am 'spoken' more than speaking, the Other speaks through me, but simply assuming this fact (in the sense of rejecting any responsibility) is also false, a case of self-deception – psychoanalysis makes me even more responsible than traditional morality, it makes me responsible even for what is beyond my (conscious) control.

This solution works on one condition: the subject (believer) is absolutely constrained by the unsurpassable horizon of its subjectivity. What Protestantism prohibits is the very thought that a believer can as it were take a position outside/above itself and look upon itself as a small particle in the vast reality. Mao was wrong when he deployed his Olympic vision reducing human experience to a tiny unimportant detail: 'The United States cannot annihilate the Chinese nation with its small stack of atom bombs. Even if the US atom bombs were so powerful that, when dropped on China, they would make a hole right through the earth, or even blow it up, that would hardly mean anything to the universe as a whole, though it might be a major event for the solar system.' There is an 'inhuman madness' in this argument: is the fact that the destruction of the planet Earth 'would hardly mean anything to the universe as a whole' not a rather poor solace for the extinguished humanity? The argument only works if, in a Kantian way, one presupposes a pure transcendental subject nonaffected by this catastrophe – a subject which, although non-existing in reality, is operative as a virtual point of reference (recall Husserl's dark dream, from his Cartesian Meditations, of how the transcendental cogito would remain unaffected by a plague that would annihilate entire humanity). In contrast to such a stance of cosmic indifference, we should act as if the entire universe was created as a backstage for the struggle of emancipation, in exactly the same way that, for Kant, God created the world in order to serve as the battleground for the ethical struggle of humanity – it is as if the fate of the entire universe is decided in our singular (and, from the global cosmic standpoint, marginal and insignificant) struggle.

The paradox is that, although (human) subjectivity is obviously not the origin of all reality, although it is a contingent local event in the universe, the path to universal truth does not lead through the abstraction from it in the well-known sense of 'let's try to imagine how the world is independently of us', the approach which brings us to some 'grey' objective structure – such a vision of 'subjectless' world is by definition just a negative image of subjectivity itself, its own vision of the world in its absence. (The same holds for all the attempts to picture humanity as an insignificant species on a small planet on the edge of our galaxy, i.e., to view it the same way we view a colony of ants.) Since we are subjects, constrained to the horizon of subjectivity, we should instead focus on what the fact of subjectivity implies for the universe and its structure: the event of subject derails the balance, it throws the world out of joint, but such a derailment is the universal truth of the world. What this also implies is that the access to 'reality in itself' does not demand from us that we overcome our 'partiality' and arrive at a neutral vision elevated above our particular struggles – we are 'universal beings' only in our full partial engagements. This contrast is clearly discernible in the case of love: against the Buddhist love of All or any other notion of the harmony with the cosmos, we should assert the radically exclusive love for the singular One, a love which throws out of joint the smooth flow of our lives.

This is also why the idea of sacrifice is foreign to Protestantism. In Catholicism, one is expected to earn salvation through earthly sacrifices, while Protestantism moves beyond this logic of exchange: there is no need for external sacrifice, a believer as empty subject ($) IS sacrifice (of all substantial content, i.e., it emerges through what mystics and Sade call the second death). This is what Catholicism doesn't see: one doesn't get anything in exchange for sacrifice, giving already IS getting (in sacrificing all its substantial content a believer gets itself, emerges as pure subject).

Here negative theology enters – as an obstacle to self-instrumentalization. Self-instrumentalization presupposes the big Other whose privileged interpreter and instrument is the revolutionary agent. Münzer belongs to this line, he even grounded it; he was wrong in founding the authentic revolutionary spirit on natural law (or a theological version of it): for him, a true believer is able to decipher the Other (his command) and to realize it, to be the instrument of his realization. Luther was right here to criticize Münzer as der Schwärmer who pretended to know the divine mind. Luther warns against such Majestätsspekulation, against trying to discern the will of god, of deus absconditus: one should abandon attempts to know what the Other wants from you and to assume your position in this world, while realizing the Other as a 'hole' in this position, a subtraction from it. God introduces the cut of the Absolute' into the ordered Aristotelian universe (thus, of course, making the latter contingent), and the tension between the two can be resolved neither through excluding one side nor by thinking a 'pactum' or a historical-dialectical relation between the two but only by thinking one (the divine Absolute) as the subtraction, the hole in the Other. Yet, in order to uphold the theological and statist reality he affirmed, Luther could not uphold the radicalism of this solution which goes much further than Münzer's. Although Münzer's notion of revolutionary activity implies that our struggle for liberation is a process that takes place in God himself, his self-instrumentalization of the revolutionary agent as an agent of divine will enables him to avoid the radical openness of the struggle, the fact that the fate of God himself is decided in our revolutionary activity.

However, Luther himself later compromised this radical position, not only for pragmatic-opportunist reasons ('I need the state support to guard against counter-reformation, therefore it is not prudent to support a revolt that is bound to fail anyway'), but also on a purely theological level: as a 'professor of old testament theology', as he was characterized, he begins to practice what Lacan called 'discourse of University' and, as a 'professor of old testament theology', as someone once said, he retreats to the Thomist-Aristotelian safe ground: 'he reverts back to a position which elides the "hole", the "subtraction" that the Other's desire (it's constitutional unknowability) rips into the fabric of the ordered (causal) world.' So we find ourselves back in a rationally ordered hierarchic universe where 'everyone is called to a station and it is sin to surpass and transgress that station'; the peasant revolt is rejected because it disturbs this well-ordered universe.

Of course Luther does not simply regress to Aquinas – he remains within the nominalist lineage and maintains the gap between deus absconditus and deus revelatus usually correlated with the difference between potentia dei absoluta and potentia dei ordinata. In the Thomist tradition, God had become rationalized to the point of nearly becoming intelligible in terms of the laws of nature which resulted in a kind of impinging of the ordered whole on the Creator. In response to these difficulties, nominalist theologians introduced a distinction between God's absolute power (potentia Dei absoluta) and God's ordained power (potentia Dei ordinata). Being utterly transcendent and mysterious, God could do anything; however, God has also entered willingly into a covenant with his people and freely binds himself to this covenant. Thus, from the point of view of God's ordained power, he is intelligible, as is of course not the case in regard to potentia Dei aboluta which thereby implies the severing of the relations of the Creator with his creation.

Since deus absconditus is beyond our rational comprehension, the temptation is to privilege mystical experience as the only contact with Him. In the predominant reading, the young Luther was a mystic, but then later, after dealing with the radical elements of the Reformation, he changed his position. But there is a basic continuity in his thought regarding mysticism: Luther did not rule out 'high mysticism' as impossible but rather cautioned against its dangers – for him, accessus has priority over raptus, i.e., justification by faith through the incarnate and crucified Word has priority over raptus by the uncreated word (the latter being that which was characterized by dangerous speculations not tethered to the Word).

Although Luther employs the concept of the potentia ordinata of God, so characteristic for nominalistic theology, he gives it a Christological point instead of its primary epistemological meaning: the potentia ordinata is for him not primarily the order established by the inscrutable free God who could as well have established another order, but the order of redemption in Jesus

Christ, established out of God's mercy to provide sinful man with a refuge from danger.[3] But is this notion of potentia ordinata not all too close to the traditional notion of a transcendent God who dwells in itself and then decides to reveal Himself to us, humans, to become God-for-us, by way of the divine Word which provides meaningful order to our existence? So what if we risk the opposite approach and conceive potentia absoluta not as some transcendent and impenetrable God of Beyond but as the 'irrational' miracle, a hole in reality – in short, as the incarnation/revelation itself. It is the Aristotelian God which is in-itself and for us, i.e., our representation of the In-itself, while Revelation is not logos (logos is the Aristotelian order) but the break of the Absolute into logos. When we are talking about God-in-itself, we should recall what Hegel says about our search for the meaning of Egyptian works of art (pyramids, Sphinx):

> In deciphering such a meaning we often, to be sure, go too far today because in fact almost all the shapes present themselves directly as symbols. In the same way in which we try to explain this meaning to ourselves, it might have been clear and intelligible as a meaning to the insight of the Egyptians themselves. But the Egyptian symbols, as we saw at the very beginning, contain implicitly much, explicitly nothing. There are works undertaken with the attempt to make them clear to themselves, yet they do not get beyond the struggle after what is absolutely evident. In this sense we regard the Egyptian works of art as containing riddles, the right solution of which is in part unattained not only by us, but generally by those who posed these riddles to themselves.[4]

It is in this sense that Hegel talks about 'objective riddle': a Sphinx is not a riddle for our finite mind but in and for itself, 'objectively', and the same holds for deus absconditus whose impenetrable mystery is a mystery for God himself. Chesterton saw this clearly – in his 'Introduction to Book of Job', he praised it as 'the most interesting of ancient books. We may almost say of the book of Job that it is the most interesting of modern books.'[5] What accounts for its 'modernity' is the way in which the book of Job strikes a dissonant cord in the Old Testament:

> Everywhere else, then, the Old Testament positively rejoices in the obliteration of man in comparison with the divine purpose. The book of Job stands definitely alone because the book of Job definitely asks, 'But what is the purpose of God? Is it worth the sacrifice even of our miserable humanity? Of course, it is easy enough to wipe out our own paltry wills for the sake of a will that is grander and kinder. But is it grander and kinder? Let God use His tools; let God break His tools. But what is He doing, and what are they being broken for?' The real surprise, however, is that in the end, the book of Job does not provide a satisfying answer to this riddle: 'it does not end in a way that is conventionally satisfactory. Job is not told that his misfortunes were due to his sins or a part of any plan for his improvement. /.../ God comes in at the end, not to answer riddles, but to propound them.[6]

And the 'great surprise' is that the book of Job:

> makes Job suddenly satisfied with the mere presentation of something impenetrable. Verbally speaking the enigmas of Jehovah seem darker and more desolate than the enigmas of Job; yet Job was comfortless before the speech of Jehovah and is comforted after it. He has been told nothing, but he feels the terrible and tingling atmosphere of something which is too good to be told. The refusal of God to explain His design is itself a burning hint of His design. The riddles of God are more satisfying than the solutions of man.[7]

In short, God performs here what Lacan calls a point de capiton: he resolves the riddle by supplanting it with an even more radical riddle, by redoubling the riddle, by transposing the riddle from Job's mind into 'the thing itself' – he himself comes to share Job's astonishment at the chaotic madness of the created universe: 'Job puts forward a note of interrogation; God answers with a note of exclamation. Instead of proving to Job that it is an explainable world, He insists that it is a much stranger world than Job ever thought it was.' So, far from providing some kind of satisfactory account of Job's undeserved suffering, God's appearance at the end ultimately amounts to pure boasting, a horror show with elements of farcical spectacle – a pure argument of authority grounded in breath-taking display of power: 'You see all what I can do? Can you do this? Who are you then to complain?' So what we get is neither the good God letting Job know that his suffering just an ordeal destined to test his faith, nor a dark God beyond Law, the God of pure caprice, but rather a God who acts as someone caught in the moment of impotence, weakness at least, and tries to escape his predicament by empty boasting. What we get at the end is a kind of cheap Hollywood horror show with lots of special effects – no wonder that many commentators tend to dismiss Job's story as a remainder of the previous pagan mythology which should have been excluded from the Bible. In his reading of the 'Book of Job', the Norwegian theologian Peter Wessel Zapffe accentuated Job's 'boundless perplexity' when God himself finally appears to him: expecting a sacred and pure God whose intellect is infinitely superior to ours, Job 'finds himself confronted with a world ruler of grotesque primitiveness, a cosmic cave-dweller, a braggart and blusterer, almost agreeable in his total ignorance of spiritual culture. /. . ./ What is new for Job is not God's greatness in quantifiable terms; that he knew fully in advance /. . ./; what is new is the qualitative baseness.'[8]

In other words, God – the God of the real – is like the Lady in courtly love, it is das Ding, a capricious cruel master who simply has no sense of universal justice. God-the-Father thus quite literally doesn't know what he is doing, and Christ is the one who does know it, but is reduced to an impotent compassionate observer, addressing his father with 'Father, can't you see I'm burning?' – burning together with all the victims of the father's rage. Only by falling into his own creation and wandering around in it as an impassive observer can god perceive the horror of his creation and the fact that the He, the highest Law-giver, is himself the supreme Criminal (as Chesterton saw it clearly in The Man Who Was Thursday).

The ultimate choice is thus: is God the big Other, a guarantor of meaning (accessible to us or beyond our reach), or a crack of the Real that tears up the texture of reality? With regard to the topic of theology and revolution, this choice means: is god a transcendent point of reference that legitimizes our instrumentalization (enabling us to claim that we act on His behalf), or is he the guarantor of ontological opening which, precisely, prevents such instrumentalization? In Badiou's terms, is the reference to God in political theology sustained by the logic of purification (a nihilist destruction of all that seems to contradict the divine message) or by the logic of separation – separation which does not mean only our separation from God on account of which God remains impenetrable to us, believers, but primarily a separation in the heart of God Himself? Incarnation is the separation of God from Himself, and for us, humans, being abandoned by God, abandoned to the abyss of our freedom, without His protective care, is when we are one with God, the god separated from itself.

A naïve counter-question: but why do we need God at all? Why not just humans leaving in a contingent open world? What is missing in this picture is the minimal theological experience described by Rowan Williams, that of being out-of-place in this world. In a primitive reading of this out-of-place, we are out of place in this world, and there is another true world. In a more radical reading, we exist because God itself is out of itself – and it is only in Protestantism that this dimension becomes visible. The triad of Orthodoxy, Catholicism, and Protestantism thus seems to correspond to the Lacanian triad of Imaginary-Symbolic-Real: the horizon of Orthodoxy is that of the imaginary fusion between man and God; Catholicism focuses on the symbolic exchange between the two poles; Protestantism asserts the 'subtracted' God of the intrusion of the Real.

Protestantism is thus totally incompatible, the New Age critical of the hubris of the so-called Cartesian subjectivity and its mechanicist dominating attitude towards nature. According to the New Age commonplace, the original sin of the modern Western civilization (or already of the Judeo-Christian tradition) is man's hubris, his arrogant assumption that he occupies the central place in the universe and/or that he is endowed with the divine right to master all other beings and exploit them for his profit. This hubris that disturbs the just balance of cosmic powers sooner or later forces Nature to re-establish the balance: today's ecological, social and psychic crisis is interpreted as the universe's justified answer to the man's presumption. Our only solution thus consists in the shift of the global paradigm, in adopting the new holistic attitude in which we will humbly assume our constrained place in the global Order of Being. . . In contrast to this commonplace, one should assert the excess of subjectivity (what Hegel called the 'night of the world') as the only hope of redemption: true evil does not reside in the excess of subjectivity as such, but in its 'ontologization', in its re-inscription into some global cosmic framework. Already in de Sade, excessive cruelty is ontologically 'covered' by the order of Nature as the 'Supreme Being of Evilness'; both Nazism and Stalinism involved the reference to some global Order of Being (in the case of Stalinism, the dialectical organization of the movement of matter). True arrogance is thus the very opposite of the acceptance of the hubris of subjectivity: it resides in the false humility, i.e. it emerges when the subject pretends to speak and act on behalf of the Global Cosmic Order, posing as its humble instrument. In contrast to this, the entire Western stance was anti-global: not only does Christianity involve the reference to a higher Truth which cuts into and disturbs the old pagan order of Cosmos articulated in profound Wisdoms, even Plato's Idealism itself can be qualified as the first clear elaboration of the idea that the global cosmic 'Chain of Being' is not 'all there is', that there is another Order (of Ideas) which suspends the validity of the Order of Being.

The feature one has to bear in mind here is the utter ambiguity of the notion of Evil: even what is commonly regarded as the ultimate Evil of our century, the cold bureaucratic mass killings in concentration camps, is split into two, Nazi holocaust and Gulag, and all attempts to decide 'which is worse' necessarily involve us in morally very problematic choices (the only way out seems to be the properly dialectical paradox that the Stalinist terror was in a way 'worse' – even more 'irrational' and all-threatening – precisely because it was 'less Evil', i.e. nonetheless the outcome of an authentic emancipatory liberation movement).

Perhaps the crucial ethical task today is to break the vicious cycle of these two positions, fundamentalist and liberal – and our last examples already shows the way out: the true ethical universality never resides in the quasi-neutral distance that tries to do justice to all concerned factions. So if, against fundamentalisms which ground ethical commitment in one's particular ethnic or religious identity, excluding others, one should insist on ethical universalism, one should also unconditionally insist on how every authentic ethical position by definition paradoxically combines universalism with taking sides in the ongoing struggle. Today, more than ever, one should emphasize that a true ethical position combines the assertion of Universalism with a militant, divisive position of one engaged in a struggle: true universalists are not those who preach global tolerance of differences and all-encompassing unity, but those who engage in a passionate fight for the assertion of the Truth that engages them.

Towards the end of A Conspiracy Of Faith (original title Flaskepost (Message In a Bottle), a 2016 Danish noir directed by Hans Petter Moland) there is a remarkable dialogue between Carl Morck, a burnt-out, terminally depressed detective, and Johannes, a handsome blonde serial killer of children who is as interested in destroying their parents' faith as in snatching their offspring. (This dialogue occurs only in the film, not in Jussi Adler-Olsen's novel on which the film is based, so I am referring to Nikolaj Arcel's scenario.)

Their final confrontation in a lone wooden sea cottage where Johannes holds enchained as prisoners Morck and the kidnapped children, a boy and a girl. After presenting himself as one of the Devil's son whose task is to destroy faith, Johannes tells Morck: 'And now... I'll take away your faith.' Morck promptly replies: 'You're wasting time. I don't believe in God. I don't believe in anything.' When Johannes then throws the young boy into the sea and keeps his head under water, Morck desperately shouts: 'Listen to me. Take me instead.' Johannes: 'You're rescuing people you've never met. Of course you have faith. I've never met anyone who's had as much faith as you.' Morck: 'Take me!' Johannes: 'Do you wish God would make you powerful enough to stop me?' When the boy seems dead, Johannes concludes: 'I think you will remember this day. You were here and it changed nothing. And God... never showed.' He then turns to the boy's elder sister, cuts off her ties with scissors, pushes the scissors into her hand, and tells her: 'Now you get this... And then you get your revenge. Then you will be his, then you will be free. Stab me. Stab me and you'll be free.' The girl refuses, silently nodding off: Johannes snaps at her 'You disappoint me.' And then tells Merck: 'Now you've seen. Now you must live.' At this moment the sound of a police helicopter above the cottage is heard, as a kind of pseudo-divine last-minute intervention ...⁹

The film's concluding moments are ambiguous: in a church Morck half-heartedly joins the prayer for the victims which celebrates the power of life over death, and when, in the very last shot of the film, he observes children playing on a green sunny meadow, he says: 'I thought what idiots they were. But maybe it's right...' – again, an ambiguity: what is right? For the innocent children to remain in their illusion? The final minutes of the film are obviously a retreat from the sharp ethical dilemma that occurs in the confrontation between Morck and Johannes. We should, of course, dismiss as ridiculous Johannes's idea of acting as the Devil's son, an idea which is meaningful only within the theological universe where there is a conflict between God and the Devil. If we follow T.S. Eliot's insight that the Devil's ultimate temptation is the reference to Good itself – 'the highest form of treason: to do the right deed for the wrong reason', as he put it in his Murder In the Cathedral – then it is Morck himself who is the true Devil's son. The Devil's ultimate trump card is not 'give way to your lust for power, enjoy life, abandon the chimera of higher ethical values!', but 'do all the noble deeds your heart tells you to do, live the highest ethical life, and be aware that there is no need for the reference to God in all this, it is your own inner nature which is your guide here, you are following the law of your heart!' – is this stance not personified in Morck's atheist readiness to sacrifice himself for others?

The crux of the matter is thus the enigma of atheism and ethics: can one be fully ethical, up to being ready to sacrifice oneself for the others, without believing in God? And, if we risk taking even a step further, what if *only* an atheist can be truly and unconditionally ethical? The point is not to ascribe to atheists some deeper belief too pure to be articulated in explicit dogmas – if there is anything good about religions, it is their dogmatic aspect. The title of the English translation of the novel and film – 'a conspiracy of faith' – is brilliant, and immediately reminds us of G.K. Chesterton's famous essay 'Defense of Detective Story' where he remarks how the detective story

keeps in some sense before the mind the fact that civilization itself is the most sensational of departures and the most romantic of rebellions. When the detective in a police romance stands alone, and somewhat fatuously fearless amid the knives and fists of a thief's kitchen, it does certainly serve to make us remember that it is the agent of social justice who is the original and poetic figure, while the burglars and footpads are merely placid old cosmic conservatives, happy in the immemorial respectability of apes and wolves. /The police romance/ is based on the fact that morality is the most dark and daring of conspiracies.[10]

Chesterton, of course, extends this logic to religion itself: orthodoxy, orthodox faith, is the most dark and daring of all conspiracies, while atheists are 'merely placid old cosmic conservatives, happy in the immemorial respectability of apes and wolves'. However, he is well aware that, in Christianity, things get more complicated: the 'conspiracy' of Christianity is that 'Christianity alone has felt that God, to be wholly God, must have been a rebel as well as a king,'[11] even more, that God himself, the origin of all things, for a moment becomes an atheist and doesn't believe in himself. Therein resides the lesson of Christianity: it is not only that we do not believe in God, but that God himself doesn't believe in himself, so that he also cannot survive as the non-substantial symbolic order, the virtual big Other who continues to believe in our place, for us. Second, only a belief which survives such a disappearance of the big Other is belief at its most radical, a wager more crazy than Pascal's: Pascal's wager remains epistemological, concerning only our attitude towards God, i.e., we have to assume that God exists, our wager doesn't concern God himself; while, for radical atheism, the wager is ontological – the atheist subject engages itself (in a political, artistic, etc. project), 'believes' in it, without relying on any guarantee. My thesis is thus double: not only is Christianity (in its core disavowed by its institutional practice) the only truly consequent atheism, it is also that atheists are the only true believers.

Perhaps the only way out of these impasses is what, in his unpublished 'secret' writings, Denis Diderot elaborated under the title of the 'materialist's credo'. In 'Entretien d'un Philosophe avec la maréchale de ***', he concluded: 'Après tout, le plus court est de se conduire comme si le vieillard existait... même quand on n'y croit pas. /After all, the most straightforward way is to behave as if the old guy exists... even if one doesn't believe it./' This may appear to amount to the same as Pascal's wager apropos the custom: even if you don't believe in it, act as if you believe... However, Diderot's point is exactly the opposite one: the only way to be truly moral is to act morally without regard to God's existence. In other words, Diderot directly turns around Pascal's wager (the advice to put your bets on the existence of God): 'En un mot que la plupart ont tout a perdre et rien a gagner a nier un Dieu renumerateur et vengeur. /In a word, it is that the majority of those who deny a remunerating and revenging God have all to lose and nothing to gain./'[12] In his denial of the remunerating and vengeful God, the atheist either loses everything (if he is wrong: he will be damned forever) or gains nothing (if he is right: there is no God, so nothing happens). It is this attitude which expresses true confidence in one's belief, and makes one do good deeds without regard to divine reward or punishment... 'As if the old guy exists...' – this old guy is, of course, God-the-Father, which recalls Lacan's formula le pere ou pire – father or worse. It is at this level that one should oppose Pascal and Diderot: while Pascal bets on God-the-Father, Diderot enjoins us to parier sur le pire, to put one's wager on the worse. In true ethics, one acts from the position of the inexistence of the big Other, assuming the abyss of the act deprived of any guarantee or support from the big Other.

Here we should bring in the fact that A Conspiracy of Faith is a Danish movie based on a Danish novel: is Morck's 'terminal depression' not a form of what Kierkegaard called 'infinite resignation', the crucial step towards the authentic religious experience? Kierkegaard's 'God' is the name for the Absolute Other against which we can measure the thorough contingency of reality – as such, it cannot be conceived as any kind of Substance, as the Supreme Thing (that would again make him part of Reality, its true Ground). This is why Kierkegaard has to insist on God's thorough 'desubstantialization' – God is 'beyond the order of Being', He is nothing but the mode of how we relate to him, i.e., we do not relate to him, he *is* this relating:

God himself is this: how one involves himself with Him. As far as physical and external objects are concerned, the object is something else than the mode: there are many modes. In respect to God, the how is the what. He who does not involve himself with God in the mode of absolute devotion does not become involved with God.[13]

The Christian passage to Holy Spirit as Love (Christ's 'whenever there will be love between the two of you, I will be there') is to be taken literally: God as the divine individual (Christ) passes into the purely non-substantial link between the individuals. This absolute devotion is enacted in the gesture of total self-renunciation: 'in self-renunciation one understands one is capable of nothing.'[14] This renunciation bears witness to the total gap that separates man from god: the only way to assert one's commitment to unconditional Meaning of Life is to relate ALL of our life, our entire existence, to the absolute transcendence of the divine, and since there is no common measure between our life and the divine, the sacrificial renunciation cannot be part of an exchange with God – we sacrifice all (the totality of our life) for nothing: 'The contradiction which arrests /the understanding/ is that a man is required to make the greatest possible sacrifice, to dedicate his whole life as a sacrifice – and wherefore? There is indeed no wherefore.'[15]

What this means is that there is no guarantee that our sacrifice will be rewarded, that it will reinstate meaning to our life – one has to make a leap of faith which, in the eyes of an external observer, cannot but appear as an act of madness (like Abraham's readiness to kill Isaac): 'At first glance the understanding ascertains that this is madness. The understanding asks: what's in it for me? The answer is: nothing.'[16] Or, to quote Michael Weston's concise formulation:

It is true that in terms of the measure an end remains, that 'eternal happiness' of which Kierkegaard speaks, for which everything must be ventured, but it is an end which can be related to only as essentially absent. As soon as one thinks about it as something that could be present, and so as a reward, one ceases to venture everything and so ceases to have a relation to it. Such an end is not the satisfaction of human capacities, since if it is to be granted all such satisfaction must be given up as a goal.[17]

The Good is thus (not unlike the Kantian Thing-in-itself) a negatively determined concept: when, in the movement of 'infinite resignation', I turn away from all temporal goods, goals, and ideals, then – to quote Simone Weil – 'my reason for turning away from them is that I judge them to be false by comparison with the idea of the good /.../ And what is this good? I have no idea – /.../ It is that whose name alone, if I attach my thought to it, gives me the certainty that the things of this world are not goods.'[18] In short, Kierkegaardian 'infinite resignation' displays the structure of what, following Freud, Lacan calls Versagung: the radical (self-relating) loss/renunciation of the very fantasmatic core of our being: first, I sacrifice all I have for the Cause-Thing which is for me more than my life; what I then get in exchange for this sacrifice is the loss of this Cause-Thing itself.[19]

However, does Borck's 'terminal depression' really reach this radical level of redoubled renunciation? There is a further step to be made. If we remain in Denmark, the finale of the last (third) season of the Danish noir series The Killing (Forbrydelsen, 2014) ends with an ethical act so shocking that it perplexed many of the series' most avid followers. The detective Sarah Lund (superbly played by Sofie Gråbøl) finally confronts the serial killer Rheinhardt, a corporate manager with high political connections. When the two of them are alone in a car, he coldly confesses to her his brutal murders but mockingly claims that she will never succeed to prosecute him; desperate for her impotence, she executes him with a gun. Following the advice of her colleague and lover who just confessed to her his love, she then illegally flies to Reykyavik to disappear forever... Her act of killing is THE killing in the series dedicated to resolving criminal killing, and it seems weirdly appropriate that the series of crime killings concludes with the killing performed by the agent of law. Is her illegal act a crime or an ethical act... or both? It has all the features of a supreme ethical act: Sarah's predicament when she commits the act is terrifying. She just reconciled with her lover with the prospect of a shared life, plus she made peace with her estranged son and happily accepted his girlfriend and their new-born child – and at this very moment when her happiness is so near, she faces the terrible choice – as Gråbøl, the actress, put it:

> It would have been so easy to kill her but Soren Sveistrup [the writer] wanted her to pay the highest price. For Lund, death isn't the highest price. Everything she wanted for happiness is within her reach and she has to give it all up in order to do the right thing.[20]

But was this the right thing to do? It certainly meets the Kantian formal criteria of an ethical act: by doing it she loses everything, personal erotic fulfilment and family happiness, plus her career is ruined and, in the eyes of the law, she becomes a criminal; plus there is no narcissistic self-satisfaction or any other »pathological« gain in doing it. She finds herself in an absolute existential void, »between the two death,« biologically alive but in away worse than dead, excluded from her community, like Antigone after she is punished by Creon. Her act is nonetheless so problematic that even those spectators who view it with some sympathy perceive it as a crazy gesture done out of despair, as an impotent outburst of revenge – here is a Guardian comment which encapsulates this common reaction:

> What we got for the woman whose moral sense of right and wrong is as solid as a continent was an ending that found her committing herself to a man who can best be described as a volatile adulterer, carrying out a cold-blooded execution, and then, to add insult to fatal injury, doing precisely what the craggy-faced fella told her to do without a jot of complaint: skipping off for a life on the run. /.../ as I watched Lund taking the battery out of her phone and flying off like a common criminal I wished they had killed her, because death would have been preferable to this ignoble end.[21]

We should nonetheless insist on the thoroughly ethical nature of her act – although this act is, if we may refer again to Kierkegaard, an ethics elevated to the level of the Religious, not unlike Abraham's readiness to kill his son, an ethics in conflict not only with the public law but with morality itself – to quote Kierkegaard, in her terrible predicament, morality itself is the temptation, that obstacle that threatens to divert her from accomplishing the proper act. Her act is criminal in the eyes of the moral big Other, but Kierkegaard's wager is that this big Other is not the ultimate point of reference of ethics. One cannot but note her the contrast with A Conspiracy of Faith, the contrast which overlaps with sexual difference: while Borck is a man ready to sacrifice himself, to lose his life, Sarah is a woman who is ready to sacrifice herself much more radically, ready to enter the 'ignoble' space of absolute loneliness, the space between the two deaths. At this razors edge where atheism and theology overlap, we get a unique form of negative theology indicated by Rowan Williams who wrote about the work of four British Catholic novelists (O'Connor, Percy, Spark, and Ellis):

> All four create a world in which the secular majority account of what is going on is severely relativized, but there is no simple alternative that anyone can step into by a single decision or even a series of decisions. The 'religious' dimension of these fictions lies in the insistent sense of incongruity, unmistakable even if no one within the fiction can say what we should be congruent with.[22]

The term 'negative theology' is usually used to designate the idea that god cannot be described by any positive determinations, so we can only circumscribe his place in a negative way – god is neither infinite nor finite, neither ideal nor real, neither being nor nonbeing, and so on. But what if, in contrast to this notion of god as a pure In-itself beyond all categorial determinations, we locate negativity into god himself, positing that the experience of the divine is, at its most elementary, a negative experience in the sense described by Williams, the experience of the out-of-jointness of our lives? At its most radical, religion is thus not the opium for the people (the opium of and for the people is today, as they say, more and more opium itself, drugs[23]), but an awareness of incongruity and/or inconsistency of existing positive reality, the incongruity which we pursued throughout this book dealing with the order of being haunted by – and originating from – its own impossibility. This ontological paradox throws a new light on the problem of deontology, of how to derive Ought from Is: some kind of deontological tension always-already is at work at the level of being itself, making it incomplete/antagonistic – the order of being is always haunted by its own impossibility, it is never what it 'ought to be'.

Only a passage through this zero-point of 'infinite resignation', of utter hopelessness, can ground a materialist ethics.

# Notes

1   Paul P. Kuennig, *Luther and Muntzer: Contrasting Theologies in Regard to Secular Authority within the Context of the German Peasant Revolt.*

2   Shamelessly quoted from https://en.wikipedia.org/wiki/Theosis_(Eastern_Christian_theology).

3   This line of thought is paraphrased from http://lutherantheologystudygroup.blogspot.si/2011/05/luther-and-potentia-ordinata-of-god.html.

4   G.W.F. Hegel, *Lectures on Fine Arts*, Part II: Chapter I. C. 3. b., quoted from www.marxists.org/reference/archive/hegel/works/ae/part2.htm#c1-c-3.

5   G. K. Chesterton, 'Introduction to the Book of Job', www.chesterton.org/gkc/theologian/job.htm.

6   G. K. Chesterton, 'Introduction to the Book of Job', www.chesterton.org/gkc/theologian/job.htm.

7   G. K. Chesterton, 'Introduction to the Book of Job', www.chesterton.org/gkc/theologian/job.htm.

8   G. K. Chesterton, 'Introduction to the Book of Job', www.chesterton.org/gkc/theologian/job.htm.

9   Department Q: A Conspiracy of Faith (2016) – IMDb, 18 March, 2022. Director: Hans Peter Moland; Writers: Nikolaj Arcel (novel) and Mikkel Norgaard (concept); Producers: Louise Vesth and Peter Aalbæk Jensen.

10 Gilbert Keith Chesterton, 'A Defense of Detective Stories,' in H. Haycraft, ed., *The Art of the Mystery Story*, New York: The Universal Library 1946, p. 6.

11 G.K. Chesterton, *Orthodoxy*, San Francisco: Ignatius Press 1995, p. 145.

12 Denis Diderot, 'Observations sur Hemsterhuis,' *Oeuvres*, Vol. I, Paris: Robert Laffont 1994, p. 759.

13 Soren Kierkegaard, *Journals and Papers*, Bloomington: Indiana University Press 1970, entry 1405.

14 Soren Kierkegaard, *Works of Love*, London: Harper Books 1962, p. 355.

15 Soren Kierkegaard, *Training in Christianity*, Princeton: Princeton University Press 1972, p. 121.

16 Soren Kierkegaard, *Journals and Papers*, entry 1608.

17 Michael Weston, *Kierkegaard and Modern Continental Philosophy*, London: Routledge 1994, pp. 85–86.

18 Quoted from Michael Weston, op. cit., p. 89. I deploy more in detail this reading of Kierkegaard in Chapter 2 of Slavoj Žižek, *The Parallax View*, Cambridge: MIT Press 2009.

19 Lacan provided a detailed interpretation of Claudel's *L'otage* in his Seminar VIII on transference (*Le seminaire, livre VIII: Le transfert*, Paris: Editions du Seuil 1982); see also my reading of *Versagung* in Chapter 2 of *The Indivisible Remainder*, London: Verso Books 1977.

20 Quoted from op. cit.

21 Quoted from www.theguardian.com/tv-and-radio/tvandradioblog/2012/dec/15/killing-iii-final-episodes. 15 December 2012.

22 Rowan Williams, *Dostoyevsky: Language, Faith and Fiction*, London: Continuum 2008, p. 6.

23 More precisely, we have today two possible reversals of Marx's claim that religion is the opium of the people: not only that the opium of the people is today more and more opium itself, but also that – as Adorno put it somewhere – in populism, 'people' itself serves as the opium of the people.

# 7

# Reformation 500: Any cause for celebration?

*John Milbank*

## 1.

The 500th anniversary of the European Reformation has not fallen in an auspicious year. In the British Isles, where arguably the divisions over this event most of all still linger (subtly and not so subtly), they have once again covertly resurfaced. The referendum vote to leave the European Union appears in many ways to repeat the old suspicion of Rome and a Protestant desire to cast adrift – to opt for an island, maritime and individualist destiny, rather than a Continental, cross-border and communitarian one. The mood may be populist, yet it oddly coincides with a British liberal revival of anti-Catholicism, culminating in the TV adaptation of Hilary Mantel's execrably tedious novel *Wolf Hall*, which sought, in denial of the facts, to render the first real modern authoritarian, Thomas Cromwell, a hero, and the Humanist Catholic martyr and genius, Thomas More, after all a sadistic villain. No doubt most of those who applauded the superb acting talents wasted on this material voted to remain in the EU – yet a significant and perhaps controlling minority of extreme liberals, in both cultural and economic terms, voted to leave. Often such people articulate a specific avowal of an Anglo-Saxon, Protestant and anarchically individualist destiny.

Viewed in more measured terms, one might regard such a supposed destiny as dubious – as a premature impulse to depart, in despair of slow reform, that tends to cause rupture, upheaval and eventually war. For just this reason, 2017 appears to be an unfortunate year in which to seek to celebrate a half-millennium of Protestantism. But another reason also is likely to render our time uncomfortable with any unqualified commemoration. This is our awareness of the danger of Wahabist and Salafist Islam. In so many ways its textual fundamentalism and iconoclasm seem akin to the spirit of the Protestant reformers – and we are bound to recall the quite staggering destruction of the medieval legacy of religious images in Britain, which had commenced earlier in Bohemia under the hands of the Hussites. No less are we bound to recall the justification of religious murder and massacre by Protestants in Ireland, Germany and elsewhere, even if this was imitated by the other side. By the same token, we have to blame also Catholics and nationalists, besides Protestants, for the many wars of religion which raged and then simmered for practically 300 years. Yet the ultimately instigating factor in these wars was the Reformation itself. Were disagreements over the Papacy and the eucharist (especially) really worth the shedding of so much blood, especially given the many intellectual and local compromises in practice that were in fact reached in many different places?

Even if we acknowledge that in some ways a military, political and iconoclastic image of the prophet Mohammed has been reinforced by Islam's experience of the West since Napoleon and its desire to exert a counter-force, then we have to recognize the iconoclastic and often terroristic aspects of the modern revolutionary legacy are themselves in a Reformation lineage.[1] As both Edmund Burke and William Cobbett contended, the paradigmatic French Revolution was in several precise ways the belated reformation of France, given the influence upon it of Jansenists, Freemasons,

Unitarian modes of belief and an apocalyptic desire to destroy and begin again.[2]

It is therefore scarcely surprising that many, including Protestants themselves, are approaching this anniversary in a muted manner. And there are also academic reasons for this muting. Over the past half-century, three different trends in historiography have contributed to a dampening of any unqualified enthusiasm for the Protestant reform. The first is the realization that we should speak, not primarily of a single 'reform', but of a long series of attempted reforms, beginning far back in the Middle Ages themselves and continuing in early modern times in the instance of the so-called 'Counter-Reformation' as well as 'the Reformation proper'. Throughout this long period there was a consistent awareness that the Church and Christendom were not just failing to live up to a Christ-like image, but were severely compromised by pervasive corruption. The Gregorian Reform itself had sought both to remove the contamination of the clerical by the secular life and to establish the supremacy of the former over the latter, in order to insist on the primacy of the spiritual and of reciprocal respect in the governing orientation of the West.[3] Yet the resultant, if unintended further secularisation of the laity, led in turn to movements meant to avert also that drift: movements of mendicant priestly involvement in the life of the people and of the poor, of many lay guilds of devotion, intercession and work, of lay communities, like those of the Beguines, seeking to combine worldly work with liturgical patterns of order and renunciation.

Yet despite all this, prevailing patterns of clerical corruption and lay dissolution remained. And reform itself might quickly turn decadent. The great English fourteenth-century alliterative epic poem, *Piers Plowman*, by William Langland, contains an intermittent denunciation of the way in which the Mendicant friars have corrupted the primacy of the parish by encouraging donation for special prayers, masses and chapels, upon which reliable stream of 'gifts' they have grown wealthy.[4] Meanwhile, more traditional monasteries, like those of the Cistercians, through the systematic employment of unlanded labourers, were starting to establish something like a proto-capitalist rural economy. Lay guilds of work could readily become exploitative monopolies of trade, while those of devotion might encourage a burgeoning trade in indulgences. Above all, papal primacy degenerated into an attempted exercise of supreme sovereign power, rather than one of spiritual persuasion.

All that might sound as if it belongs to a traditional Protestant apologetic. And it might well do so: but the point newly stressed by historians is that the Middle Ages themselves were frequently aware of all of this and in multiple ways constantly sought further reform.[5] Just for this reason, the boundary between acceptable and unacceptable reform movements was fluid: there were several sects whose charismatic and eschatological character placed them beyond the pale, yet the Franciscans and especially the spiritual Franciscans exhibited several resemblances to these (and even in rare instances to the positions of the Cathars), yet remained precariously within the embrace of Catholicism. Reformers like John Wyclif and Jan Hus were eventually ejected from the Church which they desired to renew rather than abandon, partly on the grounds that they wished to transfer the material and political dimensions of the Church into the hands of the state, yet William of Ockham sustained a roughly similar position while managing to remain within the fold, albeit in conflict with one of the popes, within a time of split papacy.

Thus to begin with, the various movements that led to the Reformation, including that of Martin Luther, were characteristically mediaeval phenomena, that might in theory have led to change rather than expulsion. They were, moreover, preceded by several humanist endeavours for reform, focused more on the lay life, on rhetoric rather than debate and ethical improvement before complex liturgical practice. These suffered a highly mixed fate – some persecution, some rejection, but also much integration on both sides of what eventually became a Catholic/Protestant divide. And although the Catholic Church itself was never to reach a compromise with the Reformers, the

Anglican Church *eventually* became, in multiple and constantly contested ways, to a degree the site of just such a compromise.

This reality of 'reform' in the plural and not in the singular is in keeping with the second new insistence on the part of historians. This is on the multiple character of 'the Reformation' itself.[6] Luther was simply one voice amongst many, and there was no theoretical or practical consistency amongst these voices. In many ways what characterizes Luther (though he was somewhat anticipated by Wyclif and Hus) is not an extremity of reforming impulse, but an abandonment of this impulse in quietist despair that falls back upon the mercy of God alone. It was just this despair of spiritual shaping which meant that it was the Lutheran and cognate reforms that received the backing of secular power, eager to exploit the consequently opening gulf of legitimacy. In turn it was this support which ensured the eventual triumph of Lutheranism and Calvinism over alternative and in a sense more genuine reforming tendencies.

For Luther, sufficient ascesis and charitable effort is now seen to be beyond the reach or even the aspiration of a totally depraved humanity. Thus a salvation that is no longer a matter of works is also no longer a matter of 're-forming' or re-shaping, at least in the first instance. It is rather a matter of faith in the grace of God who is alone righteous. The bought gifts of the mediating Church are refused, but a pure dependence on the unmediated gift of God is embraced. Already, in obliquely criticizing Wyclif, the poet and vernacular theologian Langland had seen the concealed *continuity* here: an overstress on unilateral gift, now rendered free, continues to suspend the ordinary operations of measured exchange, and so of justice, besides charity as reciprocity and relationship.[7] But other reformers in Luther's time, in partial continuity with both Langland and the German, in part vernacular theologian Meister Eckhart, had not abandoned the centrality of actual, concrete, realized human justice. Instead, they proposed the Church as a utopian just community, or else, as with the Lutheran medical reformer Paracelsus, saw faith as from the outset including a specifically 'imaginative' re-envisioning of material reality, and a kind of extended eucharistic 'working' that would liberate the secrets of nature in anticipation of the eschaton and integrally conform the human body as well as soul to a more Christomorphic shape.[8]

Reformation then, might mean 'no reform' and 'no works', at least not as the initial focus; yet it could have the very opposite meaning of 'ultra-reform' and 'much more transformative works'. This contrast is, however, too gross, and presently I will try to mediate it. For the moment, however, one can note that just as the 'no works' fork tends to mean a downgrading of the mediating human role of Mary, the Mother of God, so also the 'ultra works' fork could mean the very opposite. Thus Paracelsus' extremity of Marian devotion, allied to his Lutheran-mediated alchemical programme, led him to consider that the birth of Christ in the flesh had its eternal and celestial prototype: in consequence he reconceived the divine essence as a kind of 'goddess', corresponding to the figure of Sophia in the Bible.[9] In a folkloric and narrative account of the Trinity whose apparent heterodoxy might simply be a reflex of this idiom, Paracelsus thought that the 'monarchic' Father, from his *ungrund*, had first generated the goddess Sophia as the divine essence and then in her womb the Son and the Holy Spirit. Undoubtedly, by way of the later 'Lutheran Left', especially Valentine Weigel and Jacob Boehme, this is the ultimate source of 'sophiology' in modern theology since the nineteenth century, first with the Russians but then also more mutedly with Catholic theologians like Louis Bouyer and Hans urs von Balthasar.[10]

Of course, by highlighting Paracelsus I seem to be eccentrically looking at a supposedly marginal phenomenon in the course of a short general paper on the Reformation and its impact. But that is just the point. To begin with, there were a plethora of discontented prophets, of whom Luther and Paracelsus were but two. We must not read Luther's importance anachronistically, from the perspective of his soon to come triumph. Moreover, historiography suffers from a division of labour: the consignment of Paracelsus to the 'history of science' obscures the truth that his 'medical' thought is really a mode of lay theology and that it continued to have an enormous influence in shaping the so-called 'scientific Revolution' which, in the case of several figures like Bacon, Descartes and Hobbes was in some respects, and traceably, a secularisation and mechanization of his alchemical-eschatological vision. The same division of labour tends to mean that historians of doctrine relatively downplay tendencies, as with Paracelsus, to blend Reformation with the continued power of Renaissance pieties – not just with literary humanism and Erasmian allowance for human free will, but also with neoplatonism and Hermeticism (for example, amongst the Puritans during the English Civil War). Just such currents were also often linked with never-abandoned efforts at ecumenical reconciliation and the re-uniting of Christendom.[11]

We have seen in the first place that a reforming discontent was nothing new for the Medieval period. In the second place we have seen that, at the time of the Renaissance and Reformation, this discontent became both more multiple and more radical. The third new historiographical stress, in this case deriving from British Catholic historians like J.J. Scarisbrick and Eamon Duffy, might seem to be in tension with the first two.[12] For this is to the effect that the decadence in practice of the later Middle Ages has been much exaggerated, along with the initial popularity of the Reformation. However, there is, in the main, no contradiction: just because corruption was always prevalent in the Middle Ages, if not dominant, one can only talk, at best, about an increase in the later period. Equally, pressures for reform were usually a minority concern: most people cleaved to what they knew and found immense comfort in the parish and pictorially based modes of mediation. Furthermore, as Charles Taylor and James Simpson have stressed, insofar as reforming efforts tended to focus on morals and discipline, they tended to downplay or suppress the more ritual and above all festive aspects of popular piety.[13] In this sense religious reform ironically ran the danger of encouraging secularisation, since it unintentionally suggested the possibility of an ethical and political order without God, in a way that started to become a reality in some Renaissance Stoic and Republican thought, supremely with Machiavelli. Of course, Luther and Calvin's emphasis on faith and grace seemingly countered this ethical reduction, yet it could also reinforce it in an opposite manner, to the degree that a despair of human works and a continued suspicion of image and ritual might hand these over to a mere disenchanted pragmatic convenience.

One can, therefore, agree with Duffy and now many others, that the Reformation was not, initially, a widespread popular phenomenon – with the earlier exception of Hussitism in Bohemia where an official embrace rendered it also a matter of prodigious nationalism. In general the Reformation was more an affair of scholars and burghers, with peasants and artisans increasingly discontented for primarily material reasons, if anything attracted to the more active, 'works exacerbating' wing of reform. Nevertheless, it is arguable that Duffy and his followers tend to miss, as other scholars like Gregory, Gillespie and Pfau have indicated, the degree to which a decadent scholastic theology did tend to encourage an increasingly Pelagian and transactional approach to salvation, which underwrote the burgeoning trade in indulgences that was Luther's prime initial target.[14] The more the notion of a symbolic, participatory link between God and Creation was undone by the theologians of the *via moderna* in favour of the vision of an inscrutably powerful God laying down arbitrary conditions of redemption, the more conceptions and practices of the Church's mediation tended to become purely power-based, jurisdictional, instrumental and mercenary. If not at an entirely popular level, then at least at a vernacular one, the witnesses of Langland, of Chaucer in his *Pardoner's Tale*, of Dante, Boccaccio, Eckhart, Ruysbroeck and a host of other literary and mystical writers would seem to bear this verdict out.

## 2.

A fourth recent historical current, most represented by Brad Gregory's *The Unintended Reformation*, has blamed Protestantism for the eventual advent of secularization. This obviously counters a still far more popularly dominant narrative which regards it, to the contrary, as a beneficial harbinger of modernity. There is clearly an entire cluster of problems and cruxes involved here.

First, many secular historians have nevertheless noted tensions of the Reformation with a humanist optimism that they take to be modern. Second, if one is Protestant, one cannot straightforwardly celebrate the road from 1517 to 2017, but will either have to identify the Enlightenment as anti-Protestant or to argue that we have fatally forgotten the Protestant theological grounding of the latter. Against this background of perplexity, Gregory's thesis seems both more subtle and plausible: the Reformation's very anti-humanist despair of this world tended in the long term and unintentionally to hand it over to worldly forces. In this way, as Pierre Manent has also argued, the Reformation's pious downgrading of sacramentality in the name of transcendence proved fatal.[15] For sheer divine distance is not the concealed essence of Christianity which Protestantism finally brings to the fore; rather, as Manent argues against Marcel Gauchet, since monotheisms offer a *cult* of the hidden highest, their manifest focus must be upon a seemingly impossible and unlikely *mediation*. To try to refuse, or at least marginalize the latter, as with extreme versions of Sunni Islam, is inevitably to substitute a positive, non-negotiable and authoritarian mediation in the guise of a literally revealed divine will. But Christianity is the monotheism that, of its essence, rather most refuses this evasion, since God has drastically mediated himself through the Incarnation and its perpetuation as the Church. Insofar as Protestantism has been in danger of removing the Incarnational focus for one upon Christ's passion, transactionally regarded (and this is by no means wholly the case) then it tends simultaneously to encourage the supposed opposite of secularized disenchantment and of non-negotiable text-based fundamentalism.

However, to reach this verdict is not to say that the Reformation alone is responsible for secularization. Gregory himself, at times somewhat *sotto voce,* allows that, in theological terms, it was only building on a late scholastic legacy that was already problematic, in agreement with the longstanding theses of the Catholic scholars Louis Bouyer and Josef Lortz.[16] More recently the notion that Reformation theology was substantially both Scotist and nominalist has been challenged, but in my view with insufficient discernment of the crucial conceptual depths.[17]

It is of course the case that both Luther and Calvin, largely to their credit, reacted against the sheerly logical and rationalist style of late scholasticism. It is also the case and again to their credit, that they reacted against its semi-Pelagianism and relative downplaying of the centrality of the work of Christ in favour of a focus on the eternal divine decree.[18] For both reformers we should instead focus on the wonder of God's incarnate suffering on our behalf, in which we somehow participate, both ontologically and affectively. This was an enormous gain and involved a new Christocentricity not always maintained previously even by the Catholic mainstream, for which an ascetic and often monastic ascent to God had at times inhibited reflection on the priority of God's descent to us, in Creation as well as redemption.

Nevertheless, even in the mode of their reaction against nominalism, as found especially in the perspectives of William of Ockham and Pierre d'Ailly, the reformers scarcely escaped the terms of logical reference which those thinkers had laid down.[19] Thus nominalist semi-Pelagianism assumes that creative and created will are in some sense on the same 'concurrent' level, such that more of one means less of the other. Luther does not escape metaphysical concurrence because, in order rightly to insist on the incommensurable otherness of the divine will, he has to deny the capacity of the human will, and does not, like Aquinas, see the very effectiveness of the divine will as disclosed in its synergy with the human.[20]

A similar thing is true in the case of the doctrines of the Incarnation and the Trinity. The nominalists had struggled with the realist Patristic accounts of 'nature' in the former case and of the realist Thomist account of 'substantive relation' in the latter. A consequent insistence that God has only assumed in the Incarnation a single individual with certain properties appears to verge on Nestorianism. Equally, an insistence that the persons of the Trinity must be first identified by individual properties before relational ones – distinguished from the divine essence by a Scotist 'formal distinction' which Ockham inconsistently allows only for God – appears to verge on tritheism. By comparison, Luther proclaims that Christianity offers a 'new language' in which the normal ontological considerations do not apply: somehow the particular properties of Christ fail to coincide with his personal individuality; somehow the persons of the Trinity fully coincide with their relations which are therefore real.[21] However, this does not betoken any conversion to metaphysical realism on Luther's part, nor otherwise to a primacy of poetic, metaphorical language over logic, even though his Croatian fellow-reformer Matthias Flaccius Illyricus begins to take things in this radically humanist direction, and it is later developed by radical pietists like Oetinger and Hamann in the eighteenth century.[22] As with Paracelsus and Boehme's view that faith is also imagination, the divine power to transfigure, their contribution later shapes the spirit of Romanticism, which is in these respects less novel and modern than many suppose.

Instead, in Luther's own case, as Graham White some time ago argued, for Luther theological language is 'new', not because semantics has shifted, but because we are offered in revelation a new reality. Consequently, in a demonstrably still Ockhamist manner, for Luther God does not assume a universal human nature as such, but only the particular attributes of the individual Christ: Christ was 'thirsty, a servant, dead', but not 'thirst, servitude, death', as he puts it.[23] Nestorianism is only avoided by a radical insistence that the divine Son is the personal subject of these attributes. But in this way it would appear that the God-Man is less an ontological amalgam than simply God who has tacked onto himself a random set of isolated, individual properties. If there is, in consequence, no integrity of human nature, and indeed no divine nature apart from his singularity, then how is one to escape the monophysite conclusion that the God-Man is a pure fusion, such that human properties have become one with a divine nature that is indistinguishable from a divine individuality?

In order to avoid this reduction Calvin later insists, surely within the same nominalist, or possibly at least Scotistic *episteme*,[24] that something in the divine personhood is reserved from its involvement in the hypostatic union, as is witnessed by his 'humanist' reduction of the Patristic *communicatio idiomatum* to a mere figure of speech and his referral of the sense of this figure of exchange *solely* to the transactional exchange of substitutionary punitive atonement (as Calvin conceives it) and not to an ontological reciprocity. In this way the absolute linkage of the human and divine natures becomes merely 'improper, though not without reason', but the reason is merely the divine instrumental usage of a sheerly human sacrifice. Any Cyrilline paradox of a divine 'impassable suffering' does not figure here, as it does later in the more Thomistic Christology of the Anglican Richard Hooker. Similarly, Calvin simplistically supposes, in defiance of the imagery of Christ's eternal offering in the *Epistle to the Hebrews*, that the divine Son will eschatologically 'cease to the ambassador of the Father' and 'discharge the office of the Mediator'. This offends any notion of divine simplicity for which nothing can possibly begin or cease to happen to the divine persons or the divine nature.

To insist upon this *extra Calvinisticum* (as Lutheran scholastics later termed it) is inevitably to entertain the idea that Christ's human set of properties are set apart from the divine person and so must be in some fashion of themselves hypostasized – especially if they are not generally or universally bound together.[25] Equally, the notion that the divine person of the Son can be in any way 'reserved' from the human nature that he has assumed again implies an accidental property of the *Logos* that contradicts the divine simplicity. In this way Calvin appears (despite his apparently impeccable Chalcedonian credentials) to sustain the Nestorian tendencies of nominalist and, indeed Franciscan scholastic Christologies in general in a longer term.[26]

In the case of the Trinity, a unique reality requires for Luther that a 'new language' speak of relation as substantive. But unlike Aquinas, Luther is unable to offer any metaphysical reasons for, or inklings of such a reality – allowing of course that it escapes any complete rational grasp. He is forced to leave it as sheer surd mystery, which remains equally his only way out of the imputation of monophysitism.[27]

The same applies to his eucharistic thought which, encouraged by the reasonings of Pierre d'Ailly,[28] embraces a substantive change of the elements as 'sacramental union', yet refuses to give any sufficient metaphysical grounds for this. Insofar as he does so, then he seems, and interestingly, to regard the miracle of the Mass as a direct continuation of the Incarnation, such that the substance of Christ's body entirely perfuses the substance of the elements, just as the divine nature entirely perfuses the human one in the case of Christ's personhood. Thus Luther sarcastically asks whether the doctrine of transubstantiation would not require, by analogy, the flesh of the Virgin to be marginalized as merely 'accidental'.[29] But this analogy seems, first, to compound Luther's 'monophysite' version of the *communicatio idiomatum*, by thinking in terms of a quasi-physical 'mingling' of the natures, rather than their personal union of idiom as 'style' or personification. Secondly, to confuse a perfect integration brought about by a single divine personhood or hypostatic 'character', with one brought about by a material substance (Christ's body, which retains a human materialized soul as 'form', though not a human individuating substance), which cannot be perfectly blended with its accidents in the way that individuality or personhood can. Quite simply, Christ's body can be manifest in the modes of bread and wine (for Aquinas), but it is obviously not of its essence eatable or potable. Therefore it is inappropriate to compare the sacramental union with that of fire and iron when iron has been heated red-hot, for fire is not of its nature iron and *a fortiori* Christ's body cannot as eternal have anything 'added' to it, just as the divine nature cannot 'become' human in the Incarnation, as Luther is in danger of affirming. The folkish metaphor deployed here will simply not do the metaphysical job required.

The same metaphysical deficiency applies yet again to his account of predestination, where (as admittedly for Aquinas, who is very inadequate in this regard) he affirms salvation only by election, which involves the divine withholding of election from some sinners, yet inconsistently (again like Aquinas) denies that this implies divine election to reprobation, since if omission can ethically be commission for us, then all the more must this hold for an infinite power. Long before Calvin, Gregory of Rimini had already fully owned up to this latent grim conclusion of Western theology in the wake of Augustine's final writings.[30]

In all these instances, Luther's metaphysical undernourishment encourages a fideism that is the natural ally of authoritarianism. It could only be escaped by stronger doctrines of mystical participation, required to understand how the saved were able to enter into a Christ-space nominalistically foreclosed against any substantive or really relational sharing. Inevitably then, Lutheran Mystics like Weigel began to develop more realist modes of metaphysics, and this was even to a degree true of Protestant scholasticism.[31]

Yet it is easy to be misled here by some later apparent Protestant scholastic espousals of Thomistic analogy: a frequent primacy in their writings of the analogy of proportionality as equivalence of ratio between the divine and human can conceal an effective espousal of univocity, as can even an embrace of the primacy of attribution if this is seen in terms of efficient causal instigation by a therefore entirely unknown goodness, truth etc as opposed to a real participatory communication of a formality and a teleology.

Equally, the confinement of a general metaphysics to 'being' as univocal, and the positing of a 'special metaphysics' or 'natural theology' for God by Goclenius and others at the turn of the sixteenth century is not evidence, as Richard A.

Muller suggests, of a departure from Scotist univocity, but precisely evidence of the embrace of a new *schemata* for metaphysics which only Scotism allowed, whereby metaphysics is not equally and aporetically about God and Being, nor does God lie as cause of finite being altogether outside the scope of metaphysics, as for Aquinas, but rather he is regionally and secondarily located within the scope of a metaphysics whose subject is univocal being, even though as incommensurable infinite being he is the cause of being insofar as it is finite.[32] Where some Protestant scholastics experienced unease about this subordination of God to being, they tended, as Muller notes, to appeal to a neoplatonic notion of God as *supra-ens*, though often in such a way as to increase a rupture of sheer distance between God and his creation, since they did not usually embrace a neoplatonic emanationist *schema*.

It is also the case that the Protestant insistence on the primacy and absoluteness of the divine will meant that they tended to embrace what is, at least genealogically a Scotist account of contingency, whereby the contingent is not, as for Aquinas, simply utter dependency upon God who is alone pure necessity, but is only genuinely contingent if always shadowed by a possible 'might have been otherwise', even after the enactment of the divine decision. Antonie Vos and others have shown how pervasive this 'synchronic contingency' is for Protestant thought.[33] Vos, as Dutch Reformed, wishes to celebrate it as offering a new and valid Christian ontological paradigm, but, to the contrary, it tends to diminish God by denying the inscrutable necessity and disclosive character of all that he has done, which essentially belongs to him as an infinite simplicity to whom nothing can be really added. Once more the post-Scotist retreat from Patristic and Dominican (Albertine or Thomistic) realism involves a weakened sense of the ontological difference which threatens the divine majesty in the name of a merely onticising attempt to elevate it.

Finally, against Muller's attempted (and to a degree successful) rebuff of the common claim that Protestant thought was Scotist and univocalist, it must be insisted that Luther was metaphysically Ockhamist (in accordance with his university education)[34] and that this position assumes and indeed exacerbates univocity, not just with respect to being – where it applies to each existing thing not simply *in quid*, but also, beyond Scotus, directly *in quale*, with respect to its specifying difference – but with respect also to essential identity. For as Olivier Boulnois has argued, later medieval nominalism was built upon univocity of being and of meaning because, just as Scotus reduced 'being' to a property semantically generalized from its always particular and complete occurrences (whether as infinite or finite, substantive or accidental etc), so, also, Ockham reduced any shared quality to a nominal or (in his mature thought) mental generalization from specific instances that were always, in reality, entirely particular and contingent.[35]

It is, indeed, in part Luther's nominalistic confinement which disables him from placing the participatory at the ontological outset – instead, it tends to be for him a secondary and impenetrably mystical phenomenon. Thus, for all his Christocentricity, eventually in the evolution of his thought the forensic comes first: the interval from the ineffably individual God to us can on only be bridged by a descending decree to which we must ineluctably submit.[36] Even in the case of Christ, transmission of this decree is his 'proper' work and only 'accidentally' is he our example, as encouraging our sanctification.[37] Similarly, we must first have faith in God as all-powerful and only secondarily do we receive his love as this is revealed to us. This love is moreover dominated by God's powerful will – a love that wills, disinterestedly, our well-being and in so sense offers, as Anders Nygren realized, an erotic fusion.[38] Just by token of its agapeic unilaterality it is at first purely received without supposed taint of mutuality, despite the fact that a love received entirely prior to our loving response would be indistinguishable from a violent blow. Again here, Luther's theological conceptuality runs up against the metaphysical limits of his envisioning of causation and the infinite/finite ratio. The irony of Protestantism is that, in trying to sideline metaphysical reason, it falls victim to it, save when it realizes that it must retreat from this sidelining.

Even where metaphysical participation plays in Luther a strong secondary or even primary role, it is not clear how this can be compatible with his fundamental terminism, whose logic cannot readily (despite some recent, anachronistically 'analytic' opinions to the contrary) be separated from its metaphysics.[39] Within a fundamental, if not explicit univocal and nominalist outlook, this can even result in an *excessive* mode of participation, if there is no medium between difference and identity. In consequence, the divine presence in the world is too much seen by Luther, as Thomas Torrance argued, as God's entering within and under the spatially finite to pervade it, as if it were a kind of literally bounded receptacle or container, thereby risking a sort of panentheism.[40] Equally, the participation of the believer in Christ is seen as a repetition of the *communicatio idiomatum*, exchanging perfection with sinfulness which, if it is to be seen as more than forensic (on a Calvinist model) tends to imply, given terminist assumptions, not simply a deifying entry by humans into divine personhood (though this is sometimes the language which the earlier Luther deployed) but a mystical fusion of the corrupted and the incorrupt and of death and life.[41] The path towards a heterodox tensional fusion of even good and evil and the grounding of this in God, as with Jacob Boehme and his German Idealist successors, Schelling and Hegel, would seem here to be remotely opened up.

Calvinism was indeed more rationalist than Lutheranism and so tended to refuse a fideistic mysticism. The hypostatic union must be more explained and not left as an entirely indiscernible and miraculous fusion, even though the cost of the Calvinist mode of explanation, as we have seen, is to weaken the union itself. Relations in the Trinity must be subordinated to individual possessed properties, although that borders on heresy.[42] Substantive eucharistic presence must be denied in terms of a more spiritual real presence, despite the fact that this seems to deny the words of Christ at the last supper. Above all, double predestination must be logically embraced (and still more clearly by Calvin's followers than by Calvin himself) even though this threatens divine goodness and love and thereby the entire substance of Christianity.

What we can see, therefore, is that John Henry Newman was even more right than he realized: the Reformers were nearer to repeating Patristic-era heterodoxy than might be thought. However, this was already true of the univocalist and nominalist theology whose legacy they could not free themselves from, through lack of sufficient philosophical reflection. In either case, the problem is distortion of theology by a mutated metaphysics – even if ultimately there are theological reasons, lying often in the Franciscan legacy, for this mutation.

## 3.

We should confirm then, the entanglement of the Reformation with both univocity and nominalism. These two can be taken, as so many have now argued, as the main theoretical motors of secularization. Univocity of being at once eventually renders finite being fully self-standing and God irrelevantly remote. Nominalism disconnects and disenchants reality, rendering it at once both meaningless and the playground of divine arbitrariness and impenetrable decree. Taken together, these conclusions suggest both that the Reformation was *not* the main long term source of secularization and *equally* that it played a big part in the latter eventual outcome.

We can, very briefly, summarize the latter, as well detailed by Brad Gregory and several others.[43] Protestantism has tended to disenchant nature, often encouraging ideas of the natural world as dead mechanism or meaningless force, even though the course of later scientific research has often shown, experimentally, that this desired vision does not fully correspond to reality. Yet the vision often prevails and leaves us with an inexplicable residue of consciousness and free will. We are then tempted to reduce these psychic phenomena respectively to mere representational record and the operation of force, or else to cling to spirit in the mode of cheer choice or impulse, that can itself be equated with Newtonian motion in a void, suffering no obstacle.

Our vision of nature and of ourselves within nature has thereby become debased, to our imminent ecological and cultural peril. Equally, the Reformation debased our notion of language, to which it uniquely cleaved. It failed fully to allow that texts are only constituted within, and become readable by, complex contexts of oral tradition, shared liturgical practice and educative formation. To subtract the text of the Bible from this context as a foundational authority is falsely to suggest that it can operate unequivocally and non-enigmatically, which requires it to be denatured as a set of univocal propositions and commands, as though it were the Koran as envisaged by much Sunni orthodoxy. Since it is clearly no such kind of text, even by intention, this effectively hands its reading over to hidden mediators, to clerical forces claiming merely to read when in reality they are construing. And even they, in order to prevent hermeneutical chaos amongst their own kind, must focus mainly on the doctrine of predestination in a search for God's inscrutably elective, but literally unambiguous decree. If only a revealed text is normative and normative only a literal, then only the signs of an arbitrary eternal decree can count as to real textual content. Moreover, without mediation, the problem of application of this text to life can only mean construing life as the extension of a bleak Bible. In James Simpsons's words, 'what remains for the Christian is to search for signs of election: all of life, that is, becomes an opaque book, full of doubtful signs'.[44]

Where this authority of Protestant orthodoxy was quickly refused, then it tended to be replaced by an unmanageable plethora of individual and private authorities, imposing their own wills and desires on the text, with a resultant cultural and social chaos. The only way out then became a public appeal either to a fideistic ideology (able to organize, like Salafist Islam, in a relatively formless manner) or to the supposedly transparent text of a disenchanted nature, including human nature, as with the more Socinian and rationalist tendencies of the Reformation, which were *also* there from the outset and later *became* the enlightenment. As James Simpson puts it, 'repress the material institution and you will land up with an ideational institution'. He rightly adds that 'given the quirkiness of the human psyche, ideational institutions can be, and usually are, more punishing than material ones' and bears this out with a demonstration that the vast increase of religious persecution in the early modern period can clearly be correlated with Biblical literalism (to some extent on the Catholic as well as on the Protestant side).[45]

The same Protestant refusal of mediation resulted in various degrees of iconoclasm, strongest in first Bohemia, then the British Isles and Southern France. Just as nature became disenchanted, so too did the image: no longer a conveyance of the transcendent, it sunk to the level of mere 'art' to be regulated by taste and collected in museums. The Kantian view of beauty as a meaningless but enjoyable immanent play of the faculties is the most logical transcription of this resultant attitude. However, as James Simpson has argued, iconoclasm does not stop with the image; once commenced as a suspicion of idolatry it can, by definition, never stop, and eventually tends, as in the French Revolution to terror.[46] Idols were held to bind by their power or imagined power; liberty was thereby defined as negative freedom from idolatry. Not just the idolizing of images but soon also, after Bacon, of concepts, traditions and authorities. In the end, only the originally self-authenticating, which means the pure isolated will itself can be allowed to stand – giving us, as Simpson points out, the ultimate paradox of the 'statue of liberty', the idol of non-idolization.

What end could there ever be in sight to this since, as Kant realized, we can never be quite sure of the authenticity of our own freedom? Today the process of suspicion has ceased to distinguish the dead idol from the living image of God that is the human being – even the sacred imaging status of the latter must be torn down, and especially the confines of the body that render that image manifest: thus the ultimate as it were 'Protestant' iconoclasm is the insistence upon the absolute rights of the will over a body reduced to a possession, which must necessarily include a denial of the human status of the foetus and of the objective significance of gender difference.

Finally, if universals and relations are unreal and nothing mediates, then only money, increasingly torn away from sign and image, can truly do so. Not Luther himself, but Calvin and other reformers gradually lifted the restrictions on usury and the social obligation to ensure just prices and wages. A world without value and a world of total human fallen depravity is a world that can only be governed by contract and convention, supply and demand. This is now a self-governing world without God, but it was originally, for a post-Protestant vision, a world that God was held to govern by the perverse means of passion tempering passion, vice tempering vice. As Brad Gregory has argued, the Protestant vision of a world naturally abandoned to pleasure tends to ensure in the long run the eventuation of just such a world, given a despair of the reprobate and a limited account of how far the redeemed can recover fallen nature, or even the relevance to eternally ultimate concerns of doing so.

Nevertheless, not even in the modern period is Protestantism the only, or necessarily even the main vehicle of secularization. As Eamon Duffy has argued, after John Bossy, the early modern Catholic Church departed, as much as the Reformation ones, from the high mediaeval priority of a sacramental community of fellowship, directed towards the harmonizing of society, the encouragement of social virtues and the realization of charity as a state of being in a way that gave almost as much scope to feasting as to fasting (to link this to Charles Taylor's thesis).[47] Instead, in either case, a confessionalized religion became more a matter of formal belief, prescribed rule, private beneficence and clerical surveillance. If the word was sundered by Protestants from tradition and liturgical practice, then the same applied to Catholic exercise of authority. That too, as Michel de Certeau argued, was rent from the time of development and rendered something fully present, over-against the laity, rather than something arising from them as part of the Church and coursing through them by participation.[48]

All this ensured that it fared little better with the Catholic treatment of nature, word, knowledge, image and money than with the Protestants. Catholics now tended to confine sacramentality to the lone officially sacramental seven instances, and thus Catholic natural philosophers also, like Mersenne, Gassendi and Descartes, embraced mechanisation for largely theological reasons. Albeit the Bible was at first more critically seen by Catholics like Thomas More, John Fisher and later Richard Simon as subject to historical vagaries and so in need of interpretation, this tended to be handled by rigid ecclesial imposition of meaning outside any allowance, before Newman (significantly first an Anglican) of the reality of organic development.[49] Faith was in consequence here also sundered from reason and the latter remained equally captivated by a Scotist and Suarezian conception of metaphysics, idolizing God as merely the highest being rather than Being as such, corralling the finite from the infinite and nature from grace.

As to images, they indeed proliferated all too much, but little recovery was made of an authentic sense of the iconic or theophanic, of the invisible shining through the visible, though not fully captured by it. By perpetuating and extending the mere rhetoric of instructive representation, a popular misreading of this as inviting adoration of the material image as material (which the stronger iconic vision ironically tends to avoid) was further encouraged, thereby ensuring that Protestant horror at idolatry was not altogether misplaced.

Finally, early modern Catholicism also much diluted its opposition to usury and it was Jansenists still more than Calvinists who started to shape the science that became 'political economy', largely predicated on the supposedly inevitable need for an amoral regulation of contract, transaction and the employment of Labour. The most that can be said here in mitigation is that Catholics retained marginally more than Protestants a suspicion, sometimes tending to outright critique, of modern Capitalist processes.

And it general it can be said that, while modern Catholicism has shared with Protestantism in a philosophical, theological and cultural *episteme* that has eventually engendered secularisation, it has done so in a somewhat more muted degree, more persistently recalling elements of a different Christian past.

# 4.

But is that all there is to be said about the Protestant legacy? Are we bound to reach such a *purely* negative verdict, especially if it leads to Brexit, and in its Islamic parallel version to iconoclastic destruction and righteous slaughter, of which Oliver Cromwell was already capable?[50]

I would suggest not. First, we need to mediate the contrast between Luther and the 'Lutheran left'. There is another way of reading the secondariness of works and love in Luther, especially if we allow, like Lutheran mystics, that our divine election (properly extended, after Origen, into the election of all spirits) is our very substantial, eternal reality in the light of an entirely loving God. Then we can say that doing good works and loving others are not of their true nature *reactive*: not originally designed to correct a prior bad or impaired situation, exactly as St Paul envisages the surpassing of the Law.[51] Instead, if to be justified by faith means to begin with our eternal real being which is our 'salvation' in God, then the works of love are a gratuitous extra, even though such an extra is the very being of Creation itself and even of the infinite Trinitarian God.

Regarded in this way, Protestant works are *more radical* than Catholic works. The latter can be sometimes conceived as simply trying to meet an asymptotically receding mark, or as minimally trying to make up for a deficiency. But Protestant works as 'sanctifying' aim towards perfection, as John Wesley later brought out. In this sense, they become more akin to deification in the Greek Patristic meaning as regards the individual person. But the Lutheran and later the Puritan Left tended to extend that inheritance towards a perfecting of the social and even the cosmic order – because it often preserved the Renaissance alchemical impulse, besides the more 'materialist' (non Joachite) apocalyptic tradition of the Dominican Savanorola, which intensified and optimized the Augustinian anticipation of a purer Church on the cusp of the *eschaton*, alongside an increased conflict with an increasingly debased world.[52] Since we are already eternally saved in God, we can set about restoring the world in anticipation of the Second Coming of Christ – and a world restored means a world reverted to that Edenic freshness where the first state of goodness was itself the state of the ever-new producing of further gratuitous goods.

In Luther's case, this radicalism is most apparent in his authentically antinomian ethics: we are now to do good, like God, purely creatively and expressively, solely for *the sake* of doing good and not to earn heaven or even to contain a preceding wrong.[53] We copy God's unmerited grace in this way and the proud record of Protestant charity would seem to show a significant gain here. Thus the law of the gospel is also the created, *natural* law, and Luther affirms this point more emphatically than Aquinas, who tended to underrate the *imperative* as opposed to motivational innovation of the gospel, just as nearly everyone before Luther overrated the coincidence of the Old Covenant with the law of nature.[54] For Luther, in a novel fashion, all human law-codes, even those of the Old Testament and the Church's canons are correspondingly regarded with a suspicion that recovers St Paul's antinomian recognition that all human rule-making is as marred by our fallenness, as much or more than transgression of these same regulations. Some English Protestant radicals, culminating with William Blake, sustained and elaborated this by no means necessarily heterodox recognition.

This is not to deny that there is, in the Reformation legacy, as already noted and as Blake recognised in his later writings, an undeniable loss of the Catholic sense of charity as mutual, celebratory love and reconciling community, and of the Catholic view that we cannot trust in God's grace if we are not already loving him and actively loving our neighbour.[55] Faith should not displace the primacy of charity if we are really reading St Paul.

But there is a second and equally interesting point to be made about Luther. The unintended secularization brought about by the Reformation derives, as we have seen, from its instigation of a dualism. God over against the world, grace over nature, faith over reason. As a result of the pious desire for a religious purity, the world, nature and reason are stripped of significance, left to their own sordid devices. However, although the priority of grace and the suspicion of *ascesis* are linked, these two marks of Protestantism are also in tension with each other. Grace in opposition to nature, divine action overly contrasted with human, produces duality. But the suspicion of *ascesis* does just the opposite. It rather encourages the view that there should be *no* secular/religious divide at all. That the fully religious life can be lived, as Luther and Calvin argued, and as Meister Eckhart and Johannes Tauler had already taught, in any ordinary worldly vocation, if it be honourable and honourably undertaken. Likewise, we can praise God in the vernacular and we can be as fully Christian as sexual partners and parents as we can as celibate people – even if that vocation becomes unnecessarily undervalued.

The trouble, of course, is that a spiritual vocation undertaken in a disenchanted world tends to undo itself and not really to figure as a role within the Church – such that, as many scholars have noted, the ecclesial participation of the laity was often *reduced* in the Protestant Church, compared with the medieval one (even if the familial, domestic sphere became more of a site of piety and care).[56] And the Calvinist version of redeeming the world through a Church polity, though much stronger than the Lutheran one which had handed Church jurisdiction over to the secular arm, was conceived too much in terms of Old Testament law and a chain of obedient command.

Nevertheless, in the Lutheran sense of a Christian social practice beyond the law lay the seeds of a more transformative vision. Above all, Luther had a perhaps unprecedented and intense vision of the goodness of matter and the degree to which, as of itself blameless, it had remained uncorrupted by the Fall.[57] It is considerably for this reason that he sees the Incarnation and the Eucharist as necessary sources of uncontaminated grace, and this vision encourages a later possibility of extending the importance of a purification of matter and of the human benefits thereby gained. It is in this regard that one can reconsider the Lutheran emphasis upon a theology of descent: the *theologia gloriae* is refused as the false aspiration of ascending *ascesis*; instead we are to consider and receive the divine *kenosis* in the stable, on the Cross and in the Bread and Wine.

This contrast can bring a seemingly bizarre parallel to mind: namely the contrast between a Plotinian neoplatonism of psychic ascent to the One and the theurgic neoplatonism of Iamblichus (and then Proclus and Damascius) which stressed in addition the descent of divine powers towards us in ritual acts – a perspective whose Christian variant is found in Dionysius the Areopagite and Maximus the Confessor.

Yet not so bizarre after all. Because the Lutheran left, beginning with Paracelsus, was precisely fusing a Lutheran descent with a theurgic one, under both neoplatonic and Hermetic influences. It is also such a fusion which allows descent to become more synergic and more merged with human action and working, in an, as it were 'alchemical' expansion of the priestly action of the eucharist.

In these respects, one can argue that there have also been positive consequences of the Reformation, at first unintended, but later intended, albeit by a minority, all the way from Paracelsus to William Blake, Novalis and Franz von Baader. In rather broader terms, while one can deplore indeed the loss of the human cycle of fasting and feasting, at the same time there is a sense in which it took Protestants to be yet more radically non-dualist and so more fully *Catholic* than earlier Catholic tradition. If there was a final abandonment of the theophanic image and the sacramental, then, in compensation, both could now be more radically envisaged as arising everywhere, as even the poetry of John Milton shows.[58] Thus the Anglican Thomas Traherne celebrated the abiding sacrality of the cosmos in a new way; Anglican poets and prose-writers celebrated nature for what she was in herself as well as for what she symbolized of the transcendent. Similarly, art and aesthetic theory by no means always confined art within the bounds of the divertingly beautiful, with transcendence negatively confined to the terrifying sublime, but sometimes (from the 'picturesque' to the early Romantic) now intimated a sacramental glory as breaking through all beautiful artefacts. Already indeed, the death of the icon was balanced in the seventeenth century by the rise of the enigmatic emblem, expanding the metaphoric word in the direction of the disclosively symbolic.[59]

Equally, Lutherans like Herder and Hegel allowed the lost authority of time to return by rediscovering the Biblical sacrality of the historical process and the event, as opposed to the ascetic focus on the liberation of the individual soul. Other Lutherans like Jacobi and Hamann and the originally Anglican John Henry Newman realised anew that all reason needs faith and all faith reasoning. The Danish Lutheran Søren Kierkegaard produced the beautifully non-snobbish picture of the new Abraham as a plump Copenhagen Burgher, strolling through the park on Sunday afternoon but renouncing everything in his heart just so that he may re-receive it and enjoy it as pure non-reactive gift, in a manner that perfectly fuses the Catholic with the Lutheran attitude.

Modern Catholic thought and practice has recognized all this and learnt in the end from Protestants – including the significantly once Anglican Newman, as likewise G.K. Chesterton. It has renounced Baroque neo-scholastic decadence by re-integrating nature and grace, faith and reason. It has embraced the vernacular and married life more fully. It has learnt from Protestant poetry and landscape art; it has grown tired of Cartesian mechanism and dualism in a way partially indebted to the integrating attitudes of the Puritan Cambridge Platonists and then to various Protestant German and British Romantic philosophers.

We need, therefore, an ecumenical and long-term approach when we assess the legacy of the Reformation and its relation to secularisation. A great deal of the dualism that marks Protestant thought was taken over from late Mediaeval thought, and sustained as much by Counter-Reformation as by Protestant thinkers. Similarly, while the Reformation and its legacy was in some ways a disaster that broke Europe apart, as it today incipiently remains, and blinded us to nature's real enchantment, at the same time and from the outset, it pointed in an opposite way towards a more radical cure of a much older disease and so to a more authentic mode of the Catholic.

In short, to a way of being Christian in the ordinary. Of course asceticism is required in the Christian life. But it took Protestants fully to see that individual asceticism could become another sort of idol. For if God is truly the transcendent God, then he is not an ontic *alternative* to the world that he has made, including the pervasive sexuality of all life, as if we had to choose between the two, or love creatures less by loving God more,[60] any more than created being can be redeemed if individual souls alone are rescued, without the rescue also of their fellow creatures and all the linkages between them. To go up to God is to go simultaneously outwards to the cosmos, which persists, but is transfigured, as Traherne saw. 'Further up' is also 'further in', as another Protestant writer, C. S Lewis put in, in the course of offering a Christian and Platonic vision also to children and on children's terms – yet another way in which the Protestant legacy has helped to enrich our understanding and enactment of the Catholic gospel.[61]

In short, a radicalised Orthodoxy of the future should cleave to Catholic tradition, yet learn also from the more transformative works envisaged by Protestantism, especially in its more radical and exotic varieties.

# Notes

1   See Tom Holland's remarkable British Channel 4 TV Documentary, *Isis: The Origins of Violence.*

2   William Cobbett, *A History of the Protestant Reformation in England and Ireland* (Charlotte NC: TAN books, 2012), Chap XV, §§ 429–449, pp. 354–472.

3   See Eugen Rosenstock-Huessy, *Out of Revolution: Autobiography of Western Man* (Providence: RI, 1969), 516–562; Harold J. Berman, 'The Religious Foundations of Western Law' in *Faith and Order: The Reconciliation of Law and Religion* (Grand Rapids Mich: Eerdmans, 1993), 35–53.

4   William Langland, *Piers Plowman* [B text, parallel text edition with modern translation by E. Talbot Daivdson] eds E. Robertson and S.H.A. Shepherd (W.W. Norton: New York, 2006).

5   Steve Ozment, *The Age of Reform, 1250–1550: An Intellectual and Religious History of Late Medieval and Reformation Europe* (New Haven CONN: Yale UP 1980); James Simpson, *Reform and Cultural Revolution [The Oxford Literary History Vo l2: 1350–1547]* (Oxford: OUP, 2002); Charles Taylor, *A Secular Age* (Cambridge Mass: Harvard UP, 2007), 25–218.

6   Brad Gregory, *Salvation at Stake: Christian Martyrdom in Early Modern Europe* (Cambridge MASS: Harvard UP, 2001); *The Unintended Reformation* (Cambridge MASS: Harvard UP, 2012), 1–128

7   See John Milbank and Arabella Milbank, 'I am Imagynatyf: Some Comments on David Aers' accounts of *Piers Plowman* in *Syndicate* [online journal] March 2017.

8   Andrew Weeks, *Paracelsus: Speculative Theory and the Crisis of the Early Reformation* (New York: SUNY, 1997).

9   Weeks, *Paracelsus*, 81–85.

10  See Michaal Martin, *The Submerged Reality: Sophiology and the Turn to a Poetic Metaphysics* (Kettering OH: Angelico, 2015).

11  See, for example, Francis Yates, *The Rosicrucian Enlightenment* (London: RKP, 1972). For all its inaccuracies and questionable claims, this work helped to opened up the proper investigation of the undoubted intellectual and cultural importance of 'esoteric' currents of Christianity.

12  Eamon Duffy, *The Stripping of the Altars: Traditional Religion in England, 1400–1580* (New Haven CONN: Yale UP, 1992)

13  Taylor, *A Secular Age*; Simpson, *Reform and Cultural Revolution*.

14  Gregory, *The Unintended Reformation*, 25–73; Michael Allen Gillespie, *The Theological Origins of Modernity* (Chicago: Chicago UP, 2009), 19–43; Thomas Pfau, *Minding the Modern: Human Agency, Intellectual Traditions and Responsible Knowledge* (Notre Dame Ind: Notre Dame UP, 2013) 160–213.

15  Pierre Manent, *Metamorphoses of the City*, 304–327.

16  Louis Bouyer, *The Spirit and Forms of Protestantism* (Strongsville OH: Scepter, 2001); Josef Lortz, *Reformation in Germany* (New York: Herder and Herder, 1968).

17  Richard A. Muller, 'Not Scotist: understandings of being, univocity and analogy in early-modern Reformed thought', in *Reformation and Renaissance Review*, Vol 14, No 2, 2012, 127–150.

18  D.V. N. Bagchi, 'Luther and Scholasticism' in *Protestant Scholasticism: Essays in Reassessment*, eds Carl R. Trueman and R.S. Clark (Carlisle; Paternoster Press, 1999), 3–15.

19  See Graham White, *Luther as Nominalist: A Study of the Logical Method Used in Luther's Disputations in the Light of Their Medieval Background* (Helsinki: Luther-Agricola Society, 1994).

20  Martin Luther, 'The Bondage of the Will' in Erasmus/Luther, *Discourse on Free Will* (London: Continuum, 2005), 85–115.

21  White, *Luther as Nominalist*, 299–348.

22  For Illyricus, see Debora Shuger, *Sacred Rhetoric: The Christian Grand Style in the English Renaissance* (Princeton NJ: Princeton UP, 1988), 65–106 and *passim*.

23  White, *Luther as Nominalist*, 283.

24  David C. Steinmetz, 'The Scholastic Calvin' in Trueman and Clark, *Protestant Scholasticism*, 16–30. Scotus affirmed, unlike Aquinas, a human *esse* for Christ and a continued purely human unifying formality of the human nature.

25  Calvin, *Institutes of the Christian Religion*, Book Two, Chap XIV.

26  See Aaron Riches, Ecce Homo: *On the Divine Unity of Christ* (Grand Rapids MICH: Eerdmans, 2016).

27  White, *Luther as Nominalist*, 181–230.

28  Martin Luther, 'On the Babylonian Captivity of the Church' in Timothy F. Lull ed., *Martin Luther's Basic Theological Writings* 285. D'Ailly accepted transubstantiation merely on the grounds of Church authority, which surely throws into a very dark light his chairmanship of the committee at the Council of Constance which sent Jan Hus to the stake.

29  Luther, 'On the Babylonian Captivity', 288–289.

30  Peter Martyr Vermigli was familiar with Gregory of Rimini in this respect. See Frank A. James III, 'Peter Martyr Vermigli: At the Crossroads of Late Medieval Scholasticism, Christian Humanism and Resurgent Augustinianism' in Trueman and Clark, *Protestant Scholasticism*, 62–78.

31  See Muller, 'Not Scotist'.

32  See Olivier Boulnois, *Métaphysiques rebelles; Genèse et structure d'une science au Moyen Âge* (Paris; PUF, 2013), 261–311.

33  Antonie Vos, 'Scholasticism and Reformation' in William J. van Asselt and Eef Decker eds., *Reformation and Scholasticism: An Ecumencial Enterprise* (Grand Rapids MICH: Baker Academic, 2001), 99–119.

**34** D.V. N. Bagchi, 'Luther and Scholasticism'.

**35** Olivier Boulnois, *Métaphysiques rebelles,* 343–379.

**36** For the relevant debates here, see Carl E. Braaten and Robert W. Jenson, *Union with Christ: the New Finnish Interpretation of Luther* (Grand Rapids MICH: Eerdmans, 1998).

**37** See Sun Young-Kim, *Luther on Faith and Love: Christ and the Law in the 1535* Galatians *Commentary* (Minneapolis MN: Augsburg Fortress Press, 2014).

**38** Anders Nygren, *Agape and Eros* trans Philip Watson (London: SPCK, 1983).

**39** Boulnois, *loc cit.*

**40** Thomas Torrance, *Space, Time and Incarnation* (Edinburgh: T. and T. Clark, 1997).

**41** See Sammeli Juntunen's fine article, 'Luther and Metaphysics; What is the Structure of Being according to Luther?' in Braaten and Jenson, *Union with Christ,* 129–160 esp pp. 154–155. Juntunen would not endorse my conclusion here, but he astutely points out that Luther appears trapped between metaphors of one substantial union of the human being with Christ, and other of a consubstantial 'two substances' in us, tending to a kind of schizophrenia. As he rightly says, *neither* is what Luther intends, but I would argue that he lacks a realist metaphysics which would allow him properly to understand our incorporation into Christ's divine humanity (into his human body and divine spirit) as an ever-increased sharing in his divine personhood, a non-identical repetition of his divinely articulate character. My reading is also confirmed (though again the author would deny it) by Dennis Bielfeldt's plausible objection to Juntunen (and the Finnish reading of Luther in general), that, with respect to our union with Christ, Luther is not talking about participation, but about 'the relation of being *present in*'. Bielfeldt takes this 'perichoresis' as more avoiding any dangerous confusion of the human with the substance of the infinite (failing to understand that Proclean, Thomistic and Cusan participation in the infinite substance does not involve such confusion), yet does not see, for the reasons given above in the main text, that precisely *this* model of perichoretic presence is likely to imply, in Luther's nominalistic terms, just the divine-human fusion – more *drastically* than does 'participation' – which he is trying to avoid. See Dennis Bielfeldt, 'Response to Sammi Juntunen, "Luther and Metaphysics"' in *Union with Christ,* 161–166.

**42** Calvin, *Institutes,* Chap XIII, 6: 'Now of the three substances I say that each one, while related to the others, is distinguished by a special quality'. Calvin goes on to explain that the Son is 'intermediary' Wisdom, embarrassedly rushing through his immanent eternal nature to focus on his economic function in Creation and Incarnation: 7–13. Similarly the Spirit is dynamic life (14–15) but the distinctness of this function is to be understood from his economic role (which actually can give no account of its distinctness whatsoever: that can only be articulated as substantive relation analogically intimated in the ontological structures of the Creation and especially in their grace-filled renewal – this is a more genuinely participatory account of the economic function).

**43**  Gregory, *The Unintended Reformation.*

**44**  James Simpson, *Burning to Read: English Fundamentalism and its Reformation Opponents* (Cambridge MASS: Harvard UP, 2010), 140–141; Gregory, *The Unintended Reformation,* 74–128.

**45**  James Simpson, *Burning to Read,* 142–183, 260–282. Burning for heresy had only become civil law in England in 1409, but few heretics were actually burnt before the following century. Writers like Thomas More were embarrassed in their recognition that the Church Fathers did not admit the death penalty for religious fault, and justified it in terms of the dire threat to *civil* order posed by Luther, which More linked to a misreading of Erasmian texts that he was later purportedly quite happy to have banned in favour, as Simpson points out (despite all his own Biblical scepticism), of a more draconian public policing of the reading of scripture and assurance of the dominance of single authoritative meanings.

**46**  James Simpson, Under the Hammer: Iconoclasm in the Anglo-American Tradition (Oxford: OUP, 2010).

**47**  Eamon Duffy, *Reformation Divided: Catholics, Protestants and the Conversion of England* (London: Bloomsbury, 2017), 1–15; Charles Taylor, loc. cit.

**48**  Michel de Certeau, *The Mystic Fable,* trans Michael B. Smith (Chicago: Chicago UP, 2015).

**49**  Simpson, *Burning to Read,* 10–33, 222–282. Simpson notes how Thomas More retreats in an ironically 'Protestant' fashion from his earlier Erasmian fluidity about texts, in order to confront the Protestant civil danger. But he also rightly dismisses Brian Cummings's charge that More was threatening both the Scriptural foundation of Christianity and the integrity of textual meaning. Instead More more radically sees, in the face of Protestant denial, the inextricable links of text to historical contingency, institutional transmission and oral tradition.

**50**  Robert Tombs, *The English and their History* (London: Penguin, 2015), 213–248.

**51**  See John Milbank, *The Word Made Strange: Theology, Language, Culture* (Oxford: Blackwell, 2002), Chapter 9, Can Morality be Christian?, 219–232.

**52**  Henri de Lubac emphasised that the Florentine prophet did not share the Joachite and Franciscan vision of a increasingly 'spiritual' final epoch, surpassing or at least reducing the incarnate character of the era of Christ. See Henri de Lubac, *La posterité spirituelle de Joachim de Flore: De Joachim à nos jours* (Paris: Cerf, 2014), 172–173. See also on Augustine's eschatology John Milbank, *Being Reconciled: Ontology and Pardon* (London: Routledge, 2008), 132–133. But the whole issue of a typology of eschatologies and apocalyptics in the modern era is highly complex.

**53**  Martin Luther, 'Treatise on Good Works', in *Luther's Works* (New York: Augsburg-Fortress, 1959) Vol 45, ed James Atkinson, pp. 3, 109, and 'Lectures on Galatians' in Vol 26, ed Jaroslav Pelikan, 158–163.

54  Antti Raunio, 'Natural Law and Faith: the Forgotten Foundations of Ethics in Luther's Theology' in Braaten and Jenson, *Union with Christ*, 96–122; Aquinas, *ST* II.I q. 108 a.2. Raunio extends here the respective existing insights of Gustav Wingren and Oswald Bayer.

55  See John Milbank, 'The Ethics of Honour and the Possibility of Promise', in *Proceedings of the American Catholic Philosophical Association*, Vol 82, 2008, issue on 'Forgiveness', 31–65.

56  See Duffy, The Stripping of the Altars.

57  Sammeli Juntunen, 'Luther and Metaphysics', 151; Gillespie, *The Theological Origins of Modernity*, 125–127.

58  See Regina Schwartz, Sacramental Poetics at the Dawn of Secularism: When God Left the World (Chicago; Chicago UP, 2008).

59  See Aby Warburg, *Atlas Menmosyne* (Madrid; Akal Ediciones Sa, 2010).

60  In some passages of Dante's *Commedia* it is already clear that the poet's love of Beatrice is regarded as being as equally absolute as his love for God. One can construe this as meaning that the greater our love for God, who is all in all, then the greater and less qualified become all our loves (in their differentiating intensities, since we are limited creatures) for creatures. On the occasion when I delivered this paper at Westfield House, Cambridge, Slavoj Žižek in his own paper rightly described as 'obscene' the common notion that our love for creatures should be but 'partial' when compared to our absolute love of God. But (against Žižek's unqualifiedly pro-Protestant position) one could say that an iconoclastic attitude tends to intensify such an obscene stance (the lover should supposedly not 'idolize' the beloved etc), whereas a radically incarnational one refuses it. Again, Protestantism points in two opposite directions here.

61  C. S. Lewis, *The Last Battle* (London: Harper Collins, 2002).

# Instead of postface – heterotopia of 'Re'

## Boris Gunjević

> Therefore, every scribe who has been trained for the kingdom of heaven is like the master of a household who brings out of his treasure what is new and what is old.
>
> Mt. 13:52, NRSV

According to the great historian of ideas Gerhart B. Ladner, who tried to argue with keen insight that the idea of reform is something inherent to Christianity and that reform is what Christianity is all about. For Ladner, 'the idea of reform may now be defined as the idea of free, intentional and ever perfectible, multiple, prolonged and ever repeated efforts by man to reassert and augment values pre-existent in the spiritual-material compound of the world.'[1] The idea of re-form, that is to re-create, is central to biblical theology. Reform is also written about prominently in the epistles of the Apostle Paul. St. Paul provides a unique path and offers particular tools for the reform of humankind, which is significantly distinguished from any other kind of Greco-Roman so-called renewal ideologies, as Ladner calls them. Both the Pauline and the original Christian idea of reform is different from the so-called 'cosmological renewal ideology' found in Heraclitean or Virgilian poetry. The Pauline idea of reform also differs from the 'vitalistic renewal ideology' of the Carolingian or Medieval Renaissance on one hand, and it stands in opposition to the 'millennial renewal ideology' manifested in different messianic esoteric groups, on the other. All these renewal ideologies are incomplete because they either assume returning to a preconceived idealized Golden Age, or they are strongly characterized by endless, cyclical repetitions without any hope for real change. However, despite problems and shortcomings, what is of crucial importance here in all these renewal approaches is the simple but decisive prefix 're-'.

The retrospective prefix 're-' almost always signifies a metaphysical shift in direction to the past, as Ladner portrays things. The 're-' is also oriented toward change as in the idea of re-formation. It means a modification up to the point that it even can imply varying degrees of *novum*. It can signify an unexpected newness, an element of improvement, as in Ovid's *Metamorphoses* where *reformare* simultaneously connotes a backward move and also a miraculous physical alteration. It also can refer to a rejuvenation or to the undoing of previous modification or change. Sometimes the poet Ovid and then the biblical translator Jerome (who follows Ovid closely) use the word 'transformation' to translate the Greek term *metamorphoses*, which is one of the strongest words in the Pauline ethical imperatives. Whether we talk about renovation, reactivation, reformation, restoration, or renewing in St. Paul's writings, this is almost always about the translation of the Greek word *metamorphosis* or *metaschimatisei*. Both words are translated as 'transformation' or, as Latin would like to put it, *reformari, reformini*. Reformation is not a literal repristination, because repristination is impossible as such. There is no actual turning back the clock to allow a pure 'do over'. Rather, repristination is simulacrum of repetition, sort of repetition of the same. Real repetition is always different experience of the action repeated. (Catherine Pickstock has written about that in her small beautiful book *Repetition and Identity*.) The Reformation is more a reassertion and a betterment with the element of newness, or as Ladner nicely puts it, '*metamorphoun* ... can contain the connotations of newness and improvement and those of old goodness in equal strength: in *reformare-reformatio*, especially, the prefix "re" points toward previous existence of the constitutive component of a substance or event while *forma* infers their being organized and consolidated toward new shape and "firmness".[2]

The prefix 're-' is a reminder why the idea of Reformation matters five hundred years later. Such a simple and small prefix contains in itself lots of intensity and *Stimmung*, lots of action and reaction. 'Re-' is a small but intense light for authors who are gathered in this book and who generously gave their essays to be published here. The strangeness and otherness of this 're-' is represented as a backward and forward movement, a simultaneous movement that leads us upward. Trajectory of promise and promise always processes transformation for better. This is a reason why Reformation of the sixteenth century matters and why we still write about it.

Contributions to understanding the Reformation are legion.[3] Nevertheless, one of the modest imperatives of this project is to look again at the achievements of the Reformation critically redefined and to see it with new eyes. The idea is to reread the Reformation texts, particularly Luther and consider new possible outcomes and unexpected transversal directions from his voluminous thought. Such critical redefinition will try to take a few steps beyond obvious questions related to the relevance of the Reformation such as the boilerplate 'what does the Reformation of the church mean for us today?'

The authors presented in this book seek to open possible new ways forward based on the Reformation's theological, philosophical, literary, and perhaps even political achievements. Their contribution echoing 'philosophies' in the title of this book. As mentioned above, their goal is to see with new eyes the unexpected and intriguing strangeness of Reformation discourse as one of the fundamental events that shaped the history of early Western modernity – the 'hinge of history' as the old Catholic historian Lord Acton called Luther at Worms. The Reformation opened possible routes beyond its place in the late medieval/early modern world to provide ideas, insights, schematics, procedures and structures for theological and most importantly philosophical discourse still going on in the early decades of the twenty-first century.

Scholars gathered for this project are convinced it is not necessary to celebrate the Reformation yet again (or still), especially if we truly understand already what the Reformation is all about. Rather, there are so many things to learn *and* unlearn from the pivotal movement in order to become humbler, committed, grateful, and graceful, more proactive in our thinking and less obsessed with winning and losing or with power. So, *Luther and Philosophies of the Reformation* is a book based on the committed common reflection in a form of platform open for everyone, a contribution to a conversation that, we hope, still goes on.

The essays are put in an order as they are presented for the sake of helping readers navigate through apparently very different and heterogeneous material. But one need not go strictly from beginning to end, and the essays can be read in any order the reader fancies. The book has multiple entrances, exits, and different diagonals, because it is imagined not as a single strand but as a sort of map with different routes to travel and various ways to arrive at further theological and philosophical investigations. It is not, of course, meant to be the final word from the authors but rather a contribution to a conversation. Perhaps that is the best way to present different and sometimes contrarian diagonals and directions of Reformation philosophies.

The purpose of such a project is to see the Reformation not only as a consequence of Renaissance Humanism but also as a complex ideological process of Late Medieval theology and politics rooted in a very specific and coordinated metaphysical system. Put another way, the Reformation is presented as a counterbalance to mainstream Medieval theological, philosophical, and political discourse that was reluctant to give way to competing approaches and sought instead to continue as before, even as the Reformation was prompted and fuelled by Renaissance Humanism. Furthermore, while the Reformation showed process and continuity in some aspects – all is not full stop and start differently – there is no argument that it was a radical event in other ways. It was a sort of historical, metaphysical, and political rupture – new and exciting but also bringing a kind of trauma impacting not simply Late Medieval/Early Modern philosophy at a time but also affecting Western theology and Western society in the long run. It was movement, process, rupture and trauma simultaneously.

In that sense our project is a reminder that Luther was not a sort of mythical arch-saint, second only to the apostle Paul, as it seems in some Lutheran circles. Luther is not, of course, public enemy number one when it comes to modern theology either, despite the take within some non-Lutheran Anglo-Saxon theological circles. That number one ranking as the theological and metaphysically proto-modern villain famously or infamously belongs to Luther's predecessor, the subtle doctor Duns Scotus, as we learn from John Milbank. Yet despite contemporary metaphysical nostalgia for Medieval times where everything was secure in smooth Thomistic analogical and participatory hierarchies, there is nothing romantic about that era. It is enough to point at Dantes's Divine Comedy or Giovanni Boccaccio's *The Decameron* to see how fragile is our nostalgia and how superficial is our imaginative projection into a phantasmic past. Ivan Illich summarizes it in the memorable Latin proverb that seems to explain everything: *Corruptio optima pessima* – 'The corruption of the best is the worst'. Something that was best in Christianity, such as love toward neighbour, charity, faith, hope, grace, and a festive and joyful Christian character that marked the Middle Ages, has become highly institutionalized and bureaucratized, reduced to an exercise in centralized management where believers are treated more as customers, there to serve clergy rather than the other way around. The best part of Christianity becomes its own perversion, and in order to recover that best part, the Reformation movement was introduced like medicine, therapy, or even a strong antidote. The effect of such a theological antidote dispensed in the idea of reform was not so much like soothing balm but more like one poison introduced to cleanse another, not like gentle massage but a shock treatment.

There is something deeply traumatic in the philosophical experience of the Reformation, and the only way forward is to revisit and work through this trauma again, at least if we do not want melancholy to return over and over. Or as the poet(s) (Prophet Isaiah and Friedrich Hölderlin) has said, only the spear that pierces can bring us healing. So the only way out from this proto-modern trauma is via Luther as a paradigmatic figure with his theological discourse and his proposed way of life. And it is not all joyous triumph of course, just the opposite. We have to go through Luther's personal and theological failures, deficient ontology, political defeats, anxieties, melancholy, depression, and misunderstandings. One of the greatest personal strengths of Luther was his ability to deal with failure and perhaps this is the place where we can start, not with patronizing questions – 'How should we read Luther today?' – but rather with questions in which we lay ourselves bare – 'How would Luther today read us?' Accusing Luther to be the greatest villain of modern theology is the same as accusing paramedic for performing triage without local anaesthetic instead of applying sophisticated surgery instruments in sterile theatre with full supporting medical stuff and equipment. Our present task is to go once again through the trauma of Luther's multi-layered discourse, not in order to repristinate but to articulate possible avant-garde theology for the twenty-first century.[4] In order to provide some preliminary sketches of such theology it is important to present some philosophical diagonals and line of discourse coming out of Luther's untamed thought.

This project is a small contribution toward how this might be done in a rather relaxed yet serious way. In order to do this, we will use Ivan Illich, Michel Foucault and Giorgio Agamben's methodological metaphor of the crab's perspective. A crab moves backward, but its eyes are directed forward, using its wide field of vision in order to see what is coming. Adopting the crab's perspective will protect us from becoming an academic mole, myopic and with tunnel vision, self-absorbed. In the word 'perspective' we find a root of two important concepts. One is the classical Greek *theoria* (contemplation), and the other is respect, that is, an honest consideration of another's perspective. In order to have access to the present, while at the same time being able to see widely the things that are coming, we need a constructive combination of classical *theoria* related to critical theory that is practiced with respect for others. This project looks at the Reformation from a crab perspective, as such it can be read that way. Or to be more precise, this project offers other perspectives (plural) that are able to question every other perspective including their own. This is one of the promises of Reformation founded in philosophy of promise. Such philosophy of promise reminds us that philosophy is not love towards wisdom, it is rather wisdom in love framed by promise as a way of life. Our book is about philosophies of Reformation that promotes wisdom in love.

The sorts of key ideas and significant questions examined in this collection of essays can, we hope, help strike a balance when looking at Luther's Reformation. Five hundred years in the past and counting, its effect is not yet counted out. What about its value? To be sure, the Reformation was no utopia, despite positive developments that cheered many. It also was no dystopia, although problems remained and new ones emerged. But all can certainly agree that, to take Foucault's term, the Reformation was a heterotopia, a very different place with layers of meaning and profound effects in its time and thereafter. With organized Christianity in decline in some parts of the world, and as legacy church bodies shrink, it is worth revisiting the birth-right Luther once embraced to try to understand that place, those ideas, and then to see if there might still be energy in that identity for the present and for the future.

# Notes

1   Gerhart B. Ladner, *The Idea of Reform: Its Impact on Christian Thought and Action in the Age of the Fathers*, rev. ed. (New York: Harper & Row, 1967), 35

2   Ladner, *The Idea of Reform*, 47.

3   To cite a few, the list includes John Bossy, *Christianity in the West, 1400–1700;* Brian Cummings, *The Literary Culture of the Reformation;* Lewis W. Spitz, *The Protestant Reformation;* Eamon Duffy, *The Stripping of the Altars;* James R. Payton Jr., *Getting the*

*Reformation Wrong;* Berndt Hamm, *Reformation of Faith in the Context of Late Medieval Theology and Piety;* James Simpson, *Burning to Read.*

4    In order to propose such theology, we can start at less important places in Luther's thought such as, for example, Luther's playing with paradoxes in his occasional and unsystematic writings, which is a healthy reminder that knowledge of God finally cannot be systematized once and for all (if context is not to be ignored), and every attempt to do so is a form of hubris. Another important place is Luther's humor and melancholy, his idea of repetition, and his understanding of passions, desire, joy, beauty, and defeat. We can also add his love of poetry, fables, history, and music. His radical and merciless critique of his own position rests finally on the idea that the cross probes everything, killing yet making alive. There are also very potent ideas Luther wrote about security, the importance of place, and the relational and participatory understanding of language. We can also add his love for Scripture, as well as some of his mistakes and misdirected pronouncements related to the ideas of interiority and exteriority or even segmentarity – Luther did not read Deleuze and Guattari but for him, conjunctions are more important as expressions of faith than Aristotelian syllogisms. For Luther conjunctions are expressing something of what God added to created order in form of 'and . . . and . . . and . . .'.

# INDEX

Made in the USA
Monee, IL
29 May 2024

59007826R20111